GRAPHIS EPHEMERA 1

GRAPHIS EPHEMERA 1

· ·

An International Collection of Promotional Art

Graphische Dokumente des täglichen Lebens

Le graphisme – un état d'esprit au quotidien

Edited by · Herausgegeben von · Edité par:

B. Martin Pedersen

Publisher and Creative Director: B. Martin Pedersen

Editors: Heinke Jenssen, Annette Crandall

Assistant Editor: Jörg Reimann

Art Directors: B. Martin Pedersen, Randell Pearson

Photographer: Walter Zuber

Graphis Press Corp. Zürich (Switzerland)

(Opposite) Designer: Polly Carpenter, Photographer: Terry Heffernan, Agency: Carpenter Design, Client: Dean Witter International, Country: USA

Contents · Inhalt · Sommaire

COMMENTARY BY JAN BURNEY ... 8	KOMMENTAR VON JAN BURNEY ... 8	COMMENTAIRE DE JAN BURNEY ... 8
COMMENTARY BY HERBERT LECHNER ... 14	KOMMENTAR VON HERBERT LECHNER ... 14	COMMENTAIRE D'HERBERT LECHNER ... 14
INDEX ... 208	KÜNSTLERVERZEICHNIS ... 208	INDEX ... 208
ARCHITECTS ... 18	ARCHITEKTEN ... 18	ARCHITECTES ... 18
AWARDS ... 20	AUSZEICHNUNGEN ... 20	DISTINCTIONS ... 20
BIRTH ANNOUNCEMENTS ... 24	GEBURTSANZEIGEN ... 26	ANNONCES DE NAISSANCE ... 24
CHRISTMAS CARDS ... 32	WEIHNACHTSKARTEN ... 32	VŒUX DE NOËL ... 32
DESIGNERS ... 66	DESIGNER ... 66	DESIGNERS ... 66
EVENTS ... 90	VERANSTALTUNGEN ... 90	MANIFESTATIONS ... 90
EXHIBITIONS ... 112	AUSSTELLUNGEN ... 112	EXPOSITIONS ... 112
ILLUSTRATORS ... 122	ILLUSTRATOREN ... 122	ILLUSTRATEURS ... 122
INDUSTRIAL DESIGNERS ... 126	INDUSTRIEDESIGNER ... 126	DESSINATEURS INDUSTRIELS ... 126
LANDSCAPE ARCHITECTS ... 127	LANDSCHAFTSARCHITEKTEN ... 127	PAYSAGISTE ... 127
INDUSTRY ... 128	INDUSTRIE ... 128	INDUSTRIE ... 128
MOVING ANNOUNCEMENTS ... 144	UMZUGSANZEIGEN ... 144	CHANGEMENTS D'ADRESSES ... 144
NEW YEAR'S CARDS ... 150	NEUJAHRSKARTEN ... 150	VŒUX DE NOUVEL AN ... 150
PHOTOGRAPHERS ... 164	PHOTOGRAPHEN ... 164	PHOTOGRAPHES ... 164
PRINTERS ... 172	DRUCKEREIEN ... 172	IMPRIMERIES ... 172
WEDDING ANNOUNCEMENTS ... 178	HOCHZEITSANZEIGEN ... 178	ANNONCES DE MARIAGE ... 178
VARIA ... 196	VARIA ... 196	VARIA ... 196.

REMARKS

WE EXTEND OUR HEARTFELT THANKS TO CONTRIBUTORS THROUGHOUT THE WORLD WHO HAVE MADE IT POSSIBLE TO PUBLISH A WIDE AND INTERNATIONAL SPECTRUM OF THE BEST WORK IN THIS FIELD.

ENTRY INSTRUCTIONS MAY BE REQUESTED AT:
GRAPHIS PRESS CORP.,
DUFOURSTRASSE 107,
8008 ZÜRICH, SWITZERLAND

ANMERKUNGEN

UNSER DANK GILT DEN EINSENDERN AUS ALLER WELT, DIE ES UNS DURCH IHRE BEI-TRÄGE ERMÖGLICHT HABEN, EIN BREITES, INTERNATIONALES SPEKTRUM DER BESTEN ARBEITEN ZU VERÖFFENTLICHEN.

TEILNAHMEBEDINGUNGEN:
GRAPHIS VERLAG AG,
DUFOURSTRASSE 107,
8008 ZÜRICH, SCHWEIZ

ANNOTATIONS

TOUTE NOTRE RECONNAISSANCE VA AUX DESIGNERS DU MONDE ENTIER DONT LES ENVOIS NOUS ONT PERMIS DE CONSTITUER UN VASTE PANORAMA INTERNATIONAL DES MEILLEURES CRÉATIONS.

MODALITÉS D'ENVOI DE TRAVAUX:
EDITIONS GRAPHIS,
DUFOURSTRASSE 107,
8008 ZÜRICH, SUISSE

(OPPOSITE) ART DIRECTOR: SUSAN CALDWELL DESIGNER: SUSAN CALDWELL AGENCY: THE Q DESIGN GROUP
CLIENT: NEW CANAAN SOCIETY FOR THE ARTS COUNTRY: USA

GRAPHIS PUBLICATIONS

GRAPHIS, THE INTERNATIONAL BI-MONTHLY JOURNAL OF VISUAL COMMUNICATION
GRAPHIS DESIGN, THE INTERNATIONAL ANNUAL OF DESIGN AND ILLUSTRATION
GRAPHIS ADVERTISING, THE INTERNATIONAL ANNUAL OF ADVERTISING
GRAPHIS BROCHURES, A COMPILATION OF BROCHURE DESIGN
GRAPHIS PHOTO, THE INTERNATIONAL ANNUAL OF PHOTOGRAPHY
GRAPHIS ALTERNATIVE PHOTOGRAPHY, THE INTERNATIONAL ANNUAL OF ALTERNATIVE PHOTOGRAPHY
GRAPHIS NUDES, A COLLECTION OF CAREFULLY SELECTED SOPHISTICATED IMAGES
GRAPHIS POSTER, THE INTERNATIONAL ANNUAL OF POSTER ART
GRAPHIS PACKAGING, AN INTERNATIONAL COMPILATION OF PACKAGING DESIGN
GRAPHIS LETTERHEAD, AN INTERNATIONAL COMPILATION OF LETTERHEAD DESIGN
GRAPHIS DIAGRAM, THE GRAPHIC VISUALIZATION OF ABSTRACT, TECHNICAL AND STATISTICAL FACTS AND FUNCTIONS
GRAPHIS LOGO, AN INTERNATIONAL COMPILATION OF LOGOS
GRAPHIS EPHEMERA, AN INTERNATIONAL COLLECTION OF PROMOTIONAL ART
GRAPHIS PUBLICATION, AN INTERNATIONAL SURVEY OF THE BEST IN MAGAZINE DESIGN
GRAPHIS ANNUAL REPORTS, AN INTERNATIONAL COMPILATION OF THE BEST DESIGNED ANNUAL REPORTS
GRAPHIS CORPORATE IDENTITY, AN INTERNATIONAL COMPILATION OF THE BEST IN CORPORATE IDENTITY DESIGN
GRAPHIS TYPOGRAPHY, AN INTERNATIONAL COMPILATION OF THE BEST IN TYPOGRAPHIC DESIGN
ART FOR SURVIVAL: THE ILLUSTRATOR AND THE ENVIRONMENT, A DOCUMENT OF ART IN THE SERVICE OF MAN.
THE GRAPHIC DESIGNER'S GREEN BOOK, ENVIRONMENTAL RESOURCES FOR THE DESIGN AND PRINT INDUSTRIES

GRAPHIS PUBLIKATIONEN

GRAPHIS, DIE INTERNATIONALE ZWEIMONATSZEITSCHRIFT DER VISUELLEN KOMMUNIKATION
GRAPHIS DESIGN, DAS INTERNATIONALE JAHRBUCH ÜBER DESIGN UND ILLUSTRATION
GRAPHIS ADVERTISING, DAS INTERNATIONALE JAHRBUCH DER WERBUNG
GRAPHIS BROCHURES, BROSCHÜRENDESIGN IM INTERNATIONAL ÜBERBLICK
GRAPHIS PHOTO, DAS INTERNATIONALE JAHRBUCH DER PHOTOGRAPHIE
GRAPHIS ALTERNATIVE PHOTOGRAPHY, DAS INTERNATIONALE JAHRBUCH ÜBER ALTERNATIVE PHOTOGRAPHIE
GRAPHIS NUDES, EINE SAMMLUNG SORGFÄLTIG AUSGEWÄHLTER AKTPHOTOGRAPHIE
GRAPHIS POSTER, DAS INTERNATIONALE JAHRBUCH DER PLAKATKUNST
GRAPHIS PACKAGING, EIN INTERNATIONALER ÜBERBLICK ÜBER DIE PACKUNGSGESTALTUNG
GRAPHIS LETTERHEAD, EIN INTERNATIONALER ÜBERBLICK ÜBER BRIEFPAPIERGESTALTUNG
GRAPHIS DIAGRAM, DIE GRAPHISCHE DARSTELLUNG ABSTRAKTER TECHNISCHER UND STATISTISCHER DATEN UND FAKTEN
GRAPHIS LOGO, EINE INTERNATIONALE AUSWAHL VON FIRMEN-LOGOS
GRAPHIS EPHEMERA, EINE INTERNATIONALE SAMMLUNG GRAPHISCHER DOKUMENTE DES TÄGLICHEN LEBENS
GRAPHIS MAGAZINDESIGN, EINE INTERNATIONALE ZUSAMMENSTELLUNG DES BESTEN ZEITSCHRIFTEN-DESIGNS
GRAPHIS ANNUAL REPORTS, EIN INTERNATIONALER ÜBERBLICK ÜBER DIE GESTALTUNG VON JAHRESBERICHTEN
GRAPHIS CORPORATE IDENTITY, EINE INTERNATIONALE AUSWAHL DES BESTEN CORPORATE IDENTITY DESIGNS
GRAPHIS TYPOGRAPHY, EINE INTERNATIONALE ZUSAMMENSTELLUNG DES BESTEN TYPOGRAPHIE DESIGN
ART FOR SURVIVAL: THE ILLUSTRATOR AND THE ENVIRONMENT, EIN DOKUMENT ÜBER DIE KUNST IM DIENSTE DES MENSCHEN
THE GRAPHIC DESIGNER'S GREEN BOOK, UMWELTKONZEPTE DER DESIGN- UND DRUCKINDUSTRIE

PUBLICATIONS GRAPHIS

GRAPHIS, LA REVUE BIMESTRIELLE INTERNATIONALE DE LA COMMUNICATION VISUELLE
GRAPHIS DESIGN, LE RÉPERTOIRE INTERNATIONAL DE LA COMMUNICATION VISUELLE
GRAPHIS ADVERTISING, LE RÉPERTOIRE INTERNATIONAL DE LA PUBLICITÉ
GRAPHIS BROCHURES, UNE COMPILATION INTERNATIONALE SUR LE DESIGN DES BROCHURES
GRAPHIS PHOTO, LE RÉPERTOIRE INTERNATIONAL DE LA PHOTOGRAPHIE
GRAPHIS ALTERNATIVE PHOTOGRAPHY, LE RÉPERTOIRE INTERNATIONAL DE LA PHOTOGRAPHIE ALTERNATIVE
GRAPHIS NUDES, UN FLORILÈGE DE LA PHOTOGRAPHIE DE NUS
GRAPHIS POSTER, LE RÉPERTOIRE INTERNATIONAL DE L'AFFICHE
GRAPHIS PACKAGING, LE RÉPERTOIRE INTERNATIONAL DE LA CRÉATION D'EMBALLAGES
GRAPHIS LETTERHEAD, LE RÉPERTOIRE INTERNATIONAL DU DESIGN DE PAPIER À LETTRES
GRAPHIS DIAGRAM, LE RÉPERTOIRE GRAPHIQUE DE FAITS ET DONNÉES ABSTRAITS, TECHNIQUES ET STATISTIQUES
GRAPHIS LOGO, LE RÉPERTOIRE INTERNATIONAL DU LOGO
GRAPHIS EPHEMERA, LE GRAPHISME – UN ÉTAT D'ESPRIT AU QUOTIDIEN
GRAPHIS PUBLICATION, LE RÉPERTOIRE INTERNATIONAL DU DESIGN DE PÉRIODIQUES
GRAPHIS ANNUAL REPORTS, PANORAMA INTERNATIONAL DU MEILLEUR DESIGN DE RAPPORTS ANNUELS D'ENTREPRISES
GRAPHIS CORPORATE IDENTITY, PANORAMA INTERNATIONAL DU MEILLEUR DESIGN D'IDENTITÉ CORPORATE
GRAPHIS TYPOGRAPHY, LE RÉPERTOIRE INTERNATIONAL DU MEILLEUR DESIGN DE TYPOGRAPHIE
ART FOR SURVIVAL: THE ILLUSTRATOR AND THE ENVIRONMENT, L'ART AU SERVICE DE LA SURVIE
THE GRAPHIC DESIGNER'S GREEN BOOK, L'ÉCOLOGIE APPLIQUÉE AU DESIGN ET À L'INDUSTRIE GRAPHIQUE

PUBLICATION NO. 241 (ISBN 3-85709-456-7)
© COPYRIGHT UNDER UNIVERSAL COPYRIGHT CONVENTION
COPYRIGHT © 1995 BY GRAPHIS PRESS CORP., DUFOURSTRASSE 107, 8008 ZURICH, SWITZERLAND
JACKET AND BOOK DESIGN COPYRIGHT © 1995 BY PEDERSEN DESIGN
141 LEXINGTON AVENUE, NEW YORK, N.Y. 10016 USA

PRINTED IN JAPAN BY TOPPAN PRINTING CO., LTD.

COMMENTARIES

KOMMENTARE

COMMENTAIRES

In December 1843, a young British civil servant, too busy to write letters of Christmas greeting to all his friends, commissioned the first Christmas card. According to legend, Henry Cole, who later became the first Director of the Victoria and Albert Museum, thus initiated a custom that now supports a multi-million dollar international business. □ Cole could certainly be forgiven for his failure to conduct lengthy correspondence. As well as writing children's books, he was closely involved with the development of the railways, the organization of government design schools, and the conception of his special "child," the South Kensington Museum (later the V&A). Another of his favorite causes, the Penny Post, ensured the success of his new Christmas card trend. Introduced in 1840, it enabled large sections of the population to communicate by mail. The opportunity was enthusiastically embraced during the festive season when distant friends and far-flung families made annual contact with each other. □ In our contemporary mobile society, families and friends are often separated by huge distances, but even in an era of faxes and E-mail, the sending of Christmas cards remains as popular as ever. As the 1993 exhibition at the V&A indicated, changes in the design and style of cards have been gradual and the majority of cards sent today are

JAN BURNEY IS A FREELANCE WRITER ON ARCHITECTURE AND DESIGN, BASED IN LONDON. EDUCATED AT THE UNIVERSITIES OF EDINBURGH AND SUSSEX, SHE WAS EDITOR OF *DESIGNER* MAGAZINE. SHE IS A FREQUENT CONTRIBUTOR TO *GRAPHIS* AND OTHER EUROPEAN AND AMERICAN MAGAZINES. HER MOST RECENT BOOK IS *ETTORE SOTTSASS DESIGN HERO* (HARPERCOLLINS, 1993).

not radically different, in visual spirit, from the cards dispatched by Cole in 1843. □ Cole's card was illustrated by the painter John Callcott Horsley, and his composition was inspired by the form of a church altarpiece. Within a framework of tree branches and vines, the central image of family festivity is flanked by illustrations of charitable largesse. These twin themes of merry-making and charity remained a persistent feature of Christmas cards through the Victorian period. □ Cole's card was published by his own lithography company in a hand-colored edition of one thousand and sold to the public for one shilling per card, then the price of dinner in a good restaurant. By 1850, however, the cost of cards had come down and the demand for cards provided good business for several publishing companies. By the end of the 19th century, sentimental scenes of robins, yule logs, and sleigh rides in the snow were joined by images of Father Christmas and religious illustrations. More sophisticated cards were influenced by the fashion for Japanese style and comic imagery was even beginning to creep in. □ Christmas cards remained a British phenomenon until 1874, when the American publisher Louis Prang recognized their commerical potential and began producing cards at his company in Boston. He introduced an elongat-

ed format and black background to emphasize the other bright colors and offered high monetary prizes for the winning designs in the competitions he organized. □ By the beginning of the 20th century, Christmas card production had become a highly profitable business, although in recent years a high proportion of consumers have been choosing to send cards with the proceeds going to charity. Many cards are now also printed on recycled paper. In terms of style, the kitsch conventions of traditional cards have been challenged by fine art and cartoon imagery. Illustration for, and sometimes by, children is also popular. Arthur Rackham and Beatrix Potter are among the many illustrators who have created designs for Christmas cards. □ The custom of sending cards at Christmas continues to flourish in a multi-media age. Cole would undoubtedly be delighted that the tradition he established in 1848 now provides a form of patronage for artists of all descriptions. □ The Victoria and Albert Museum at South Kensington, London SW7 2RL is open Tuesday through Sunday from 9.00 a.m. to 5.50 p.m., and Mondays from 12.00 to 5.50 p.m. Many of the cards on display in the exhibition were taken from the George Buday collection comprising over ten thousand cards, which he left to the museum after his death. ■

....

Im Dezember 1843 gab ein junger britischer Staatsbeamter, der keine Zeit hatte, all seinen Freunden zu Weihnachten Briefe zu schreiben, die erste Weihnachtskarte in Auftrag. Er hiess Henry Cole und sollte später der erste Direktor des Victoria and Albert Museum werden. Nach der Überlieferung war er es, der mit seinem Auftrag einen Brauch ins Leben rief, der inzwischen zum Gegenstand eines internationalen Multimillionen-Dollar-Geschäfts geworden ist. □ Man kann Cole kaum übelnehmen, dass er keine Zeit für ausgedehnte Briefwechsel fand. Er schrieb nicht nur Kinderbücher, sondern war auch in die Entwicklung des Schienenverkehrs involviert, in den Aufbau staatlicher Designschulen, und er arbeitete am Konzept seines «Lieblingskindes», des South Kensington Museum (später V&A). Ein anderes Lieblingsprojekt von ihm, die «Penny Post», verhalf dem neuen Weihnachtskartenbrauch zum Durchbruch. Diese Post wurde 1840 eingeführt und ermöglichte grossen Teilen der Bevölkerung, per Post zu kommunizieren, und von dieser Gelegenheit wurde vor allem während der Weihnachtszeit begeistert Gebrauch gemacht, um einmal jährlich Kontakt mit Freunden in der Ferne oder mit weit verstreuten Verwandten aufzunehmen. □ In unserer mobilen Gesellschaft sind Familien und Freunde oft durch riesige Distanzen getrennt, und trotz Fax und E-Mail ist das Versenden von Weihnachtskarten so beliebt wie je zuvor. Eine Ausstellung im V&A Museum 1993 war der Weihnachtskarte gewidmet, und hier konnte man feststellen, wie sich Gestaltung und Stil der Karten nur ganz allmählich verändert haben. Die Mehrzahl der heutigen Karten ist in ihrer visuellen Botschaft gar nicht so weit entfernt von den Karten, die Cole 1843 verschickte. □ Coles Karte war von dem Illustrator und Maler John Callcott Horsley illustriert, und

seine Komposition war von der Form eines Kirchenaltarbildes inspiriert. Umrahmt von Ästen und Reben wird das zentrale Motiv des Familienfestes von Illustrationen wohltätiger Grosszügigkeit begleitet. Diese Kombination von Fröhlichkeit und Wohltätigkeit blieb während der ganzen Viktorianischen Epoche ein fortwährendes Thema. □ Coles Karte wurde von seiner eigenen Lithographenanstalt in einer handkolorierten Auflage von 1000 Stück herausgegeben und für einen Shilling pro Karte verkauft, ein Betrag, den man damals für ein Abendessen in einem guten Restaurant bezahlte. Bereits 1850 jedoch war der Preis für die Karten auf einem annehmbaren Niveau, und die Nachfrage wurde für viele Verlage ein gutes Geschäft. Gegen Ende des 19. Jahrhunderts fand man ausser den sentimentalen Illustrationen von Rotkehlchen, geschmückten Tannen und Schlittenfahrten im Schnee auch Bilder des Weihnachtsmanns und religiöse Darstellungen. Anspruchsvollere Karten waren von der Begeisterung für den japanischen Still beeinflusst, und sogar der Comicstil schlich sich ein. □ Bis 1874 blieben Weihnachtskarten ein britisches Phänomen, dann erkannte der amerikanische Verleger Louis Prang ihr kommerzielles Potential, und er begann, in seiner Firma in Boston Karten zu produzieren. Er führte das längliche Format ein und den schwarzen Hintergrund, der die anderen Farben leuchten liess, und er organisierte Wettbewerbe für die Gestaltung und Illustration von Weihnachtskarten, deren Gewinner mit ansehnlichen Geldpreisen ausgezeichnet wurden. □ Zu Beginn des 20. Jahrhunderts war die Weihnachtskartenherstellung bereits ein äusserst einträgliches Geschäft, obwohl viele Verbraucher in den letzten Jahren dazu übergegangen sind, Karten zu kaufen, deren Erlös für wohltätige Zwecke verwendet wird. Viele Karten sind

....

JAN BURNEY LEBT ALS FREIE JOURNALISTIN IN LONDON. IHRE FACHGEBIETE SIND ARCHITEKTUR UND DESIGN. SIE SCHREIBT REGELMÄSSIG FÜR *GRAPHIS* UND ANDERE EUROPÄISCHE UND AMERIKANISCHE ZEITSCHRIFTEN UND WAR REDAKTEURIN DES MAGAZINS *DESIGNER*. IHR NEUSTES BUCH «ETTORE SOTTSASS: DESIGN HERO» IST 1993 ALS PAPERBACK BEI HARPERCOLLINS ERSCHIENEN.

heute auf wiederverwertetes Papier gedruckt. Was den Stil angeht, so machen heute Kunst- und Comics den eher kitschigen Motiven der konventionellen Karten Konkurrenz. Illustrationen für Kinder – und manchmal von ihnen – sind ebenfalls sehr beliebt. Arthur Rackham und Beatrix Potter behören zu den vielen Illustratoren, die Entwürfe für Weihnachtskarten gemacht haben. □ Der Brauch, Weihnachtskarten zu verschicken, floriert nach wie vor, auch im Multimedia-Zeitalter.

Cole wäre zweifellos glücklich festzustellen, dass die von ihm 1848 ins Leben gerufene Tradition eine Form der Unterstützung für Künstler aller Art bedeutet. □ Das Victoria & Albert Museum, South Kensington, London SW7 2RL ist von Dienstag bis Sonntag zwischen 9.00 und 17.50 Uhr geöffnet, Montags von 12.00–17.50 Uhr. Ein grosser Teil der Ausstellung im V&A stammte aus der Sammlung des Museums – über 10 000 Karten aus dem Nachlass des Sammlers George Buday. ■

En décembre 1843, un jeune fonctionnaire britannique, qui ne trouvait pas le temps d'écrire des lettres pour adresser ses vœux de Noël à l'ensemble de ses amis, fit réaliser ce qui devait constituer la première carte de Noël. La légende veut que ce même Henry Cole, qui devint plus tard le premier conservateur du Victoria and Albert Museum, fut ainsi l'instigateur d'une coutume qui génère aujourd'hui un volume d'affaires de plusieurs millions de dollars. □ On pourra sans doute facilement pardonner à Mr. Cole de ne pas avoir voulu assumer une correspondance trop volumineuse. Tout en écrivant des livres pour enfants, il participa activement au développement des chemins de fer et à la mise en place des premières écoles publiques d'arts décoratifs sans oublier la conception de cet «enfant» très spécial qui fut le sien, à savoir le South Kensington Museum (qui devait devenir ensuite le Victoria and Albert Museum). C'est également l'une des causes auxquelles il s'est dévoué – le système de la «poste à deux sous» – qui a permis à la nouvelle tendance des cartes de Noël de rencontrer un franc succès. Instauré en 1840, ce système offrit au plus grand nombre la possibilité de communiquer par courrier et, durant la période des fêtes, cette nouvelle opportunité fut accueillie avec beaucoup d'enthousiasme par les amis que la distance séparait et les familles éparpillées qui purent ainsi reprendre contact chaque année. □ Aujourd'hui, au sein de notre société vouée à la mobilité, les familles et les amis sont souvent séparés par de très longues distances et malgré les communications par télécopie ou par courrier électronique, l'envoi de cartes de voeux demeure une coutume très largement pratiquée. Comme en a témoigné l'exposition de 1993 tenue au Victoria and Albert Museum, les changements de style et de conception des cartes de voeux ont été très progressifs et la plupart des cartes expédiées aujourd'hui ne sont pas radicalement différentes, dans leur inspiration visuelle, de celles qu'a pu adresser Mr. Cole en 1843. □ La carte de Cole avait été illustrée par le peintre John Callcott Horsley dont la composition puisait son inspiration dans la forme du retable d'une église. Encadrée par un décor de branches d'arbre et de vignes, l'image centrale de la fête de famille côtoyait des représentations évoquant l'abondance et la générosité. Ce double thème de la réjouissance et de la charité est resté la caractéristique prédominante des cartes de Noël durant toute l'époque victorienne. □ La carte de Cole a été publiée par sa propre entreprise de lithographie

en mille exemplaires peints à la main puis proposée au public au prix d'un shilling la carte, ce qui, à l'époque, était le prix d'un dîner dans un bon restaurant. Toutefois, dès 1850, le prix des cartes régressa à un niveau beaucoup plus raisonnable et la demande croissante du public permit à plusieurs sociétés d'édition de connaître un excellent développement. A la fin du 19ème siècle, les images sentimentales de rouge-gorge, de bûches de Noël et de traîneaux sur fond de neige furent complétées par des représentations du Père-Noël et des scènes religieuses tandis que des cartes plus sophistiquées, influencées par le style japonais, mais aussi les premières représentations humoristiques firent leur apparition. □ Les cartes de Noël demeurèrent un phénomène typiquement britannique jusqu'en 1874. C'est alors qu'un éditeur américain du nom de Louis Prang prit conscience de leur potentiel commercial et lança une production de cartes dans son entreprise de Boston. □ Il introduisit un nouveau format allongé ainsi qu'un fond noir destiné à mettre en valeur les autres couleurs vives utilisées et organisa des concours de dessin avec attribution de prix d'un montant alléchant aux vainqueurs. □ Dès le début du vingtième siècle, la production des cartes de Noël est devenue une activité extrêmement lucrative. On note toutefois qu'au cours de ces dernières années, les consommateurs ont opté pour des cartes avec attribution des recettes des ventes à des organismes de charité. De même, nombre de cartes sont aujourd'hui imprimées sur du papier recyclé. En matière de graphisme, le style très kitsch des cartes traditionnelles a été quelque peu battu en brèche par les illustrations artistiques et les dessins humoristiques. Les dessins pour enfants, et parfois même réalisés par des enfants, ont aussi gagné en popularité. Arthur Rackham et Beatrix Potter font partie des nombreux créateurs spécialisés dans les illustrations pour cartes de Noël. □ A l'heure de la communication multimédia, la tradition de la carte de Noël est toujours aussi vivante. Cole serait très certainement ravi de constater que cette coutume instaurée en 1843 équivaut aujourd'hui à une forme de mécénat pour bon nombre d'artistes aux tendances les plus variées. □ Le musée Victoria and Albert de South Kensington à Londres est ouvert du mardi au dimanche de 9.00 à 17.50 heures et le lundi de 12.00 à 17.50. Une grande partie de l'exposition de cartes de Noël du V&A provient de la collection particulière du musée qui comporte un fonds de plus de 10 000 cartes du collectionneur George Buday. ■

JAN BURNEY TRAVAILLE COMME JOURNALISTE LIBRE À LONDRES. DES DOMAINES DE PRÉDILECTION SONT L'ARCHITECTURE ET LE DESIGN. ELLE PUBLIE RÉGULIÈREMENT DES ARTICLES DANS LE MAGAZINE GRAPHIS AINSI QUE DANS D'AUTRE REVEUS EN EUROPE ET AUX ETATS-UNIS. SON DERNIER OUVRAGE INTITULÉ «ETTORE SOTTSASS: DESIGN HERO» EST PARUE EN 1993 CHEZ HARPERCOLLINS.

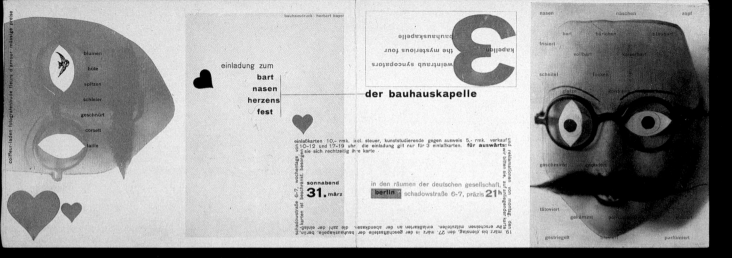

HERBERT BAYER: INVITATION TO A BAUHAUS PARTY, 1928. ORIGINAL IN THE BAUHAUS ARCHIVES. PHOTO BY ATERLIER SCHNEIDER, BERLIN.

Although seldom shown to juries or published in annuals, and only by exception found in artists' portfolios and monographs, these small and often delightful works of art fulfill the communicative function from which the entire branch lives. Ephemera! A collective name for all of those varied and fleeting trivialities that cannot really be considered a commission, but which must be completed nevertheless. Occasions—studio openings, movings, marriages, birth announcements—are as justifiable as the common greeting cards (New Year's, Easter, birthdays, Christmas). □ Whoever earns his living in the realization of creative ideas cannot avoid ephemera. Indeed, the real artist is ambitious enough to deal with such minor matters alone, resolving them in the spirit of Kurt Tucholsky who admitted that "my modest need for prose I write myself." Indeed, ephemera often reflect very personal matters that are only meant for a circle of good friends and valued acquaintances. □ Thus begins a Sisyphean task, which bears no relation to the size of the finished greeting—if it is to be finished at all! There are enough examples of occasions where great opportunities were missed—the marriage gone astray, the newborn now in school, the creative team disbanded. (No, dear reader, I am not really alluding to you in particular!) □ Once captured by

HERBERT LECHNER WAS EDITOR-IN-CHIEF OF THE TRADE MAGAZINE *GRAPHIK VISUELLES MARKETING* FOR FIVE YEARS. SINCE 1986, HE HAS WORKED AS A FREELANCE JOURNALIST IN MUNICH, FREQUENTLY WRITING ABOUT "VISUAL CULTURE." HE IS A PARTNER IN BASSE & LECHNER, A SMALL PUBLISHING FIRM SPECIALIZING IN LIMITED EDITIONS. HE IS THE AUTHOR OF SEVERAL BOOKS, INCLUDING *THE HISTORY OF MODERN TYPOGRAPHY* AND *CARTOONS AND CARICATURES IN ADVERTISING.*

the challenge of self-expression in small format, the artist begins a game of roulette, tossing between designing and discarding, a game that can rapidly become a mania. If client and designer are one and the same, then the designer suddenly starts to appreciate his own clients again, because another person is seldom as critical as one is of oneself. Somehow it seems so easy—like jumping through a burning hoop while balancing on a tightrope, snarling lions and spectators waiting below. Still, the skill of the artist is also in smiling, and in making everything appear quite easy. □ How fortunate that the painful birth of the finished card is not revealed. ("Ah that one, that was a quick sketch..." can only be heard in the late hours amongst trusted friends. And then these colleagues, shaken by similar problems, nod knowingly: "Of course.") □ Like diamonds (which are known to grow only under enormous pressure), the diminutive form of these truly precious objects emerges from the creative process. The wealth of ideas invested is breathtaking. There is hardly a technique, hardly a material, hardly a gag missing from this struggle for a "small" resolution to a problem. Postcards of Plexiglas and hand-finished wooden boxes, printed silk scarves and books in miniature. To paraphrase Goethe, "the master reveals himself in limitation." Did our classical writers also set down texts for Christmas cards? How skillfully the seemingly limited possibilities are played out. □ But in this case, a little can also mean a great deal. Alone the simple card, which is offered here in its manifold variations is remembered as distinct, amusing, and evocative. Does the direct marketer ever receive such praise? □ The old standby, paper, is still the preferred material for every kind of ephemeron. Through folding and twisting, punching and pleating, not only the designer's inclination to play is satisfied, but that of the recipient as well. Origami is wisely considered an art form by the Japanese. □ The recipient is pleased, smiles, keeps the card for a while, perhaps contemplates it once more, and then it disappears as new and other small sensations claim his attention. Nevertheless, are these endearing and passing gems not worth all our effort and commitment? To paraphrase Schiller: "Man plays only there where he is a human being in the full sense of the word, and he is only a complete human being in the place where he plays." (He did indeed write texts for Christmas cards!) ■

....

Ganz selten tauchen sie einmal bei Jurierungen und in Jahrbüchern auf, auch in den Mappen und Monographien der Künstler sind sie nur in Ausnahmen zu finden. Und das, obwohl sie in vielen Fällen kleine, bezaubernde Kunstwerke sind und ausserdem die kommunikative Aufgabe, von der die gesamte Branche lebt, am reinsten erfüllen: Ephemera! Sammelbegriff für all' jene buntgemischten und schnell vergänglichen Nebensächlichkeiten, die eigentlich keinen Auftrag darstellen, aber eben doch verfertigt werden müssen. Anlässe gibt es in Hülle und Fülle – Ateliereröffnung, Umzug, Geburtsanzeigen und immer wieder Glückwunschkarten (Neujahr, Weihnachten, Ostern, Geburtstage und die Reaktionen auf die Ephemera der lieben Kollegen). □ Wer sein Geld mit gestalterischen Ideen und ihrer Umsetzung verdient, der entkommt ihnen nicht, denn natürlich legt man seinen Ehrgeiz darein, solche Kleinigkeiten eben mal selbst zu erledigen, ganz im Sinne von Kurt Tucholsky: «Ich schreibe mir meinen kleinen Bedarf an Prosa lieber selber». Ausserdem sind es ja ganz persönliche Anliegen, die hier einem Kreis guter Freunde, lieber Bekannter, wichtiger Kontakte vermittelt werden sollen, wem sollte man die schon überlassen? □ Doch damit beginnt eine Sisyphusarbeit, die in keinem Verhältnis zur Grösse des fertigen Grusses steht. Wenn er denn fertig wird! Es gibt Beispiele, da ist der Anlass passé – die Ehe auseinander, das Neugeborene schulpflichtig, die Studio-Gemeinschaft zerbrochen –, bevor noch der grosse Wurf gelungen ist. (Nein, nein, verehrter Leser, ich habe wirklich nicht auf Sie speziell angespielt.) □ Ephemer sind diese Objekte nämlich zumeist nur für den Empfänger. Für den Kreativen, einmal gepackt von der Herausforderung der Selbstdarstellung im Kleinformat, beginnt ein Roulettespiel zwischen Entwerfen und Verwerfen, das schnell zur Manie werden kann. Sind Auftraggeber und Ausführender identisch, dann lernt man plötzlich wieder seine Kunden schätzen. Denn so kritisch – im ganzen Doppelsinn des Wortes – wie man selbst, ist wohl kein anderer. Dabei scheint es doch so einfach – etwa so, wie auf dem Hochseil durch einen brennenden Reifen zu springen, während unten zähnefletschende Löwen und Zuschauer warten. Die Kunst des Artisten besteht eben auch darin, zu lächeln und alles ganz leicht wirken zu lassen. □ Welch ein Glück, dass niemand dem fertigen Kärtchen diese Geburtswehen mehr ansieht. (Nur im ganz vertrauten Kollegenkreis hört man zu fortgeschrittener Stunde mal ein «Ach, das, das hab ich schnell so hinskizziert». Und die Kollegen, von ähnlichen Problemen geschüttelt, nicken wissend: «Genau».) □ Dabei lässt die kleine Form wahre Pretiosen der kreativen Szene entstehen, sozusagen Diamanten (die bekanntlich auch nur unter immensem Druck wachsen!) Der investierte Einfallsreichtum ist atemberaubend. Kaum eine Technik, kaum ein Material, kaum ein Gag fehlt beim Ringen um die kleine Lösung. Postkarten aus Plexiglas und handgefertigte Holzkistchen sind ebenso zu finden wie bedruckte T-Shirts und Kleinstbücher. In der Beschränkung zeigt sich erst der Meister – haben unsere Klassiker eigentlich auch Weihnachtskarten getextet? –, denn wie gekonnt wird hier mit den scheinbar knappen Möglichkeiten gespielt. □ Aber auch wenig ist da schon sehr viel: Allein die schlichte Karte, welche Variationsbreite wird hier aufgeboten, um unverwechselbar, witzig und eindrucksvoll in Erinnerung zu bleiben. Bekommen eigentlich die Direkt Marketer nie solche Grüsse? □ Wie geduldig das gute alte Papier ist – nach wie vor der liebste Grundstoff für Ephemera jeder Art –, das erweist sich aber erst, wenn noch eine Dimension

....

HERBERT LECHNER WAR FÜNF JAHRE CHEFREDAKTEUR DER FACHZEITSCHRIFT *GRAPHIK VISUELLES MARKETING*. ER ARBEITET HEUTE ALS FREIER AUTOR UND TEXTER IN MÜNCHEN. ER HAT VERSCHIEDENE BÜCHER VERÖFFENTLICHT, UNTER ANDEREM ÜBER »DIE GESCHICHTE DER MODERNEN TYPOGRAPHIE« UND ÜBER »CARTOONS UND KARIKATUR IN DER WERBUNG«.

dazukommt: Mit Falten und Falzen, Stanzen und Staunen wird nicht nur der eigene Spieltrieb, sondern auch der des Empfängers befriedigt – ein entscheidender Gesichtspunkt. Nicht umsonst gilt Origami bei den weisen Japanern als Kunstform. Manche dieser filigranen Kunstwerke offenbaren allerdings schon in ihrer Zerbrechlichkeit, dass Ephemera halt nicht für die Ewigkeit gemacht sind. □ Der Empfänger freut sich, schmunzelt, hebt das Kärtchen eine Weile

auf, zeigt es vielleicht sogar noch einmal her – doch dann ist es verschwunden, und neue, kleine Sensationen verlangen seine Aufmerksamkeit. Und trotzdem: Sind diese liebenswerten, vergänglichen Kostbarkeiten nicht all unserer Mühen und unseres Engagements wert? Denn, so Schiller: «Der Mensch spielt nur, wo er in voller Bedeutung des Wortes Mensch ist, und ist nur da ganz Mensch, wo er spielt.» (Also hat er doch Weihnachtskarten getextet!) ∎

Il est plutôt rare de les voir dans des compilations annuelles ou soumises à l'appréciation des jurés; dans les monographies et les cartons à dessin des artistes, elles ne sont pas non plus légion. Souvent, elles n'en sont pas moins de petits chefs-d'œuvre exquis qui remplissent au mieux les tâches de communication dont vit une branche tout entière: Ephemera! Tel est le terme générique désignant toutes ces créations secondaires, aussi variées qu'éphémères, qui ne représentent pas un contrat en soi, mais nécessitent cependant un travail de conception. Et ce ne sont pas les occasions qui manquent : inauguration d'un atelier, déménagement, mariage, faire-part de naissance et, encore et toujours, les cartes de vœux (Nouvel-An, Pâques, les anniversaires, Noël). □ Quiconque gagne sa vie grâce à son génie créatif, à ses idées et à leur réalisation n'y échappe pas. En effet, on n'est pas peu fier de réaliser soi-même ce genre de «bricole» lorsque l'occasion se présente. Kurt Tucholsky abondait d'ailleurs dans ce sens: «Je préfère rédiger moi-même le peu de prose dont j'ai besoin.» En outre, il s'agit de messages strictement personnels que l'on transmet à des amis intimes, à des connaissances ou à des relations importantes. Pourquoi donc s'en remettre à quelqu'un d'autre ? □ Mais c'est là que commence un véritable travail de Titan qui n'a aucun rapport avec l'œuvre parachevée – si ce stade devait être atteint un jour! Parfois, avant même d'avoir réussi un coup de maître, l'occasion appartient déjà au passé – les heureux mariés sont au chapitre du divorce, le nouveau-né est en âge de scolarité et les cohabitants du studio ne cohabitent plus. (Détrompez-vous, cher lecteur, ce n'est pas à vous en particulier que je m'adressais.) □ Éphémères, ces objets ne le sont en général que pour le destinataire. Pour le créatif, c'est une autre paire de manches. Une fois qu'il s'est laissé emballer par le défi de faire sa propre mise en scène en version petit format, commence alors un vrai casse-tête chinois entre ébauche et rejet, une opération qui peut se répéter maintes fois jusqu'à l'obsession. Si le mandant se trouve être également l'exécutant, on en vient tout à coup à apprécier ses clients. On n'est jamais aussi critique qu'envers soi-même, n'est-ce pas? Et pourtant, cela paraît si simple, comme de sauter à travers un cerceau en feu, tel un funambule, pendant que plus bas, à ses pieds, une horde de lions, tous crocs dehors, et les spectateurs attendent... Or, tout l'art de l'artiste consiste aussi à sourire, à donner l'impression que, oui, finalement c'est un jeu d'enfant. □ Quelle chance que personne n'assiste aux douleurs, aux contractions qui accompagnent la naissance de la petite carte. (Seuls quelques bons collègues au parfum ont l'occasion d'entendre, une fois que l'heure de la délivrance approche, «Oh, ce n'est rien de fracassant, j'ai juste fait une esquisse, comme ça.» Et ces mêmes collègues, tracassés par les mêmes problèmes, opinent du chef, en toute connaissance de cause: «Mais oui, c'est ça.») □ Toujours est-il que ces petits formats se transforment en objets précieux, en diamants pour ainsi dire (qui ne voient le jour, comme chacun sait, que sous une pression énorme!). Mais que de trouvailles! De quoi rester pantois. Aucune technique, aucun matériau, aucune astuce n'a été ignorée dans cette lutte acharnée pour vaincre, trouver la «mini-solution». Cartes postales en plexiglas, petites boîtes en bois réalisées à la main, carrés de soie imprimés, livres miniature, tout y est. «C'est dans l'indigence que l'on reconnaît le vrai maître» – les auteurs clasiques allemands ont-ils eux aussi rédigé des cartes de vœux pour Noël? –, car avec quelle maestria on s'est adonnés au jeu, avec des moyens apparemment limités. D'un petit rien naissent des merveilles: une carte toute simple se décline ici à l'infini, changements de format ou de tout autre paramètre, pour rester gravée dans la mémoire, faire sourire, devenir unique. En admirant ces petits chefs-d'œuvre, on peut se demander si les ténors du marketing direct reçoivent de temps à autre de tels messages? □ Pour découvrir les trésors de patience que recèle ce bon vieux papier – numéro un incontesté en matière d'annonces ou de faire-part, toutes catégories confondues –, il faut cependant lui ajouter une dimension: c'est en le pliant, en le repliant, en l'estampant, en s'étonnant que l'on satisfait son instinct du jeu, mais aussi celui du destinataire, un aspect qui ne manque pas d'intérêt. Au contraire. Si les sages japonais considèrent l'origami comme un art, ce n'est certainement pas un hasard. La fragilité de certains de ces chefs-d'œuvre filigranes est bien la preuve que toutes ces petits messages éphémères ne sont pas voués à l'éternité. □ Le destinataire se réjouit, sourit d'un air béat, soulève un instant la carte, va peut-être même jusqu'à la montrer, puis, la laisse disparaître, d'autres sensations exigeant alors toute son attention. Et pourtant: ces délicatesses passagères, chaleureuses, ne méritent-elles pas tous nos efforts, notre engagement? Pour citer Schiller encore une fois: «L'homme ne joue que lorsqu'il est homme dans tout le sens du terme et il n'est vraiment homme que lorsqu'il joue.» (Je le savais, il a bien rédigé des cartes de vœux pour Noël!) ∎

HERBERT LECHNER A ÉTÉ CINQ ANS RÉDACTEUR EN CHEF DU MAGAZINE SPÉCIALISÉ *GRAPHIK VISUELLES MARKETING*. IL EST AUJOURD'HUI ÉCRIVAIN ET RÉDACTEUR INDÉPENDANT À MUNICH. IL A PUBLIÉ ENTRE AUTRES UNE HISTOIRE DE LA TYPOGRAPHIE MODERNE ET UNE ÉTUDE SUR L'EMPLOI DE LA B.D. ET DE LA CARICATURE DANS LA PUBLICITÉ.

Standard
architecture

Stan
dard

arch
itec
ture

Jean et Aline Harari

69, rue du Faubourg Saint
Antoine
75011 Paris

Téléphone : 43 42 50 54
Fax : 43 47 23 15

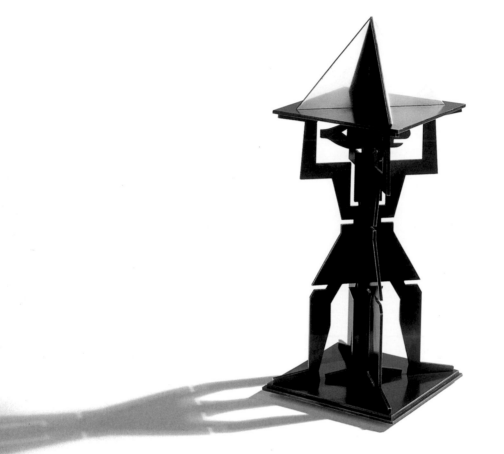

(ABOVE) ART DIRECTORS: LYNN TRICKETT, BRIAN WEBB DESIGNERS: LYNN TRICKETT, BRIAN WEBB, ANDREW THOMAS
ILLUSTRATOR/STUDIO/CLIENT: TRICKETT & WEBB LIMITED COUNTRY: GREAT BRITAIN □ (OPPOSITE) CREATIVE
DIRECTOR: KAN TAI-KEUNG ART DIRECTOR: EDDY YU CHI KONG DESIGNER: JOYCE HO NGAI SING AGENCY: KAN
TAI-KEUNG DESIGN & ASSOCIATES LTD. CLIENT: KOWLOON-CANTON RAILWAY CORPORATION COUNTRY: HONG KONG

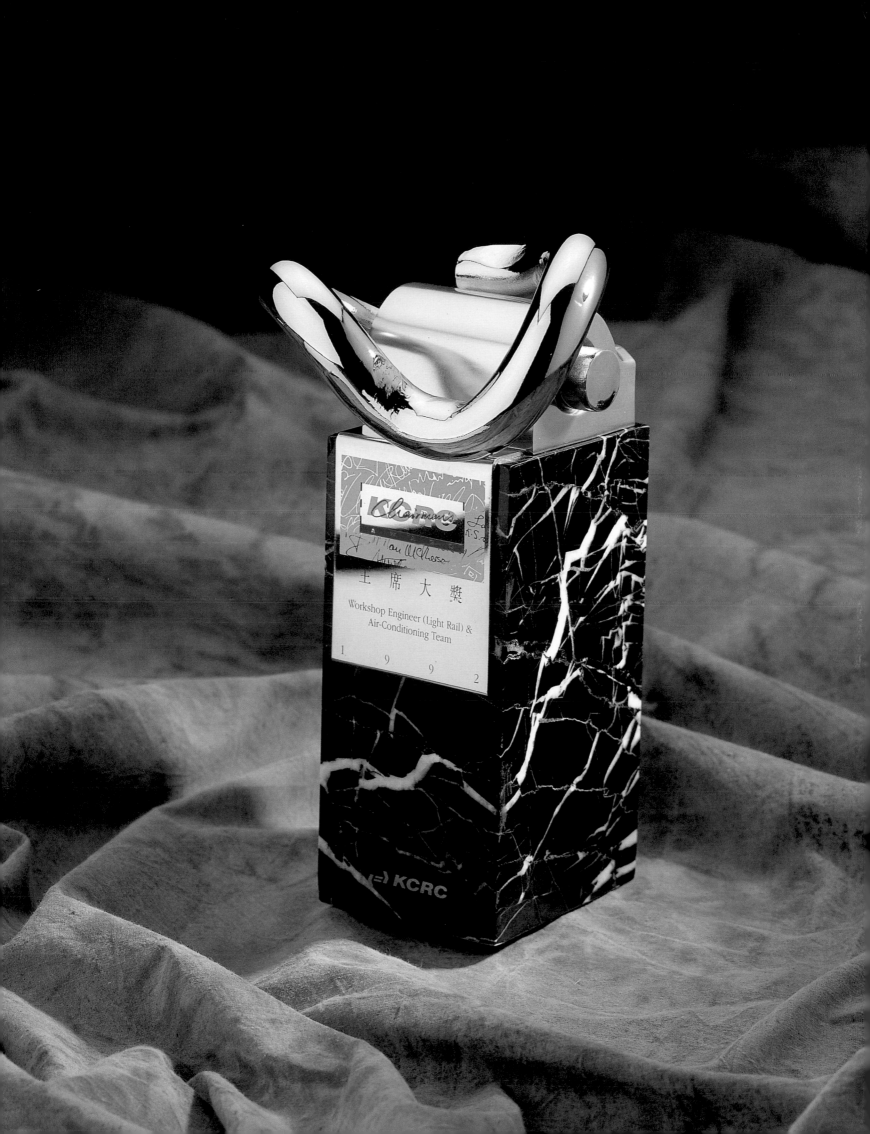

(OPPOSITE) ART DIRECTOR/DESIGNER: STEVEN JOSEPH AGENCY: SPATCHURST DESIGN ASSOCIATES CLIENT: SYDNEY ELECTRICITY COUNTRY: AUSTRALIA □ (THIS PAGE) ART DIRECTOR/DESIGNER: JOHN SAYLES COPYWRITER: WENDY LYONS AGENCY: SAYLES GRAPHIC DESIGN CLIENT: ORDER OF THE GLOBE COUNTRY: USA

23

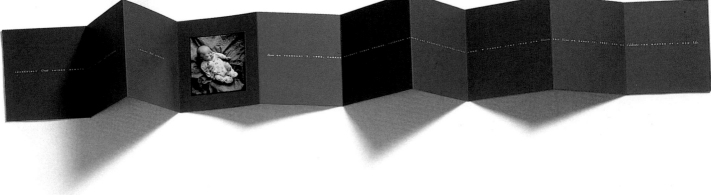

(ABOVE) ART DIRECTORS/DESIGNERS: PAT SAMATA, GREG SAMATA PHOTOGRAPHER: MARC NORBERG AGENCY: SAMATA ASSOCIATES
COUNTRY: USA ☐ (OPPOSITE) ART DIRECTOR/DESIGNER/PHOTOGRAPHER: JOHN CLARK AGENCY: STUDIO JOHN CLARK COUNTRY: USA

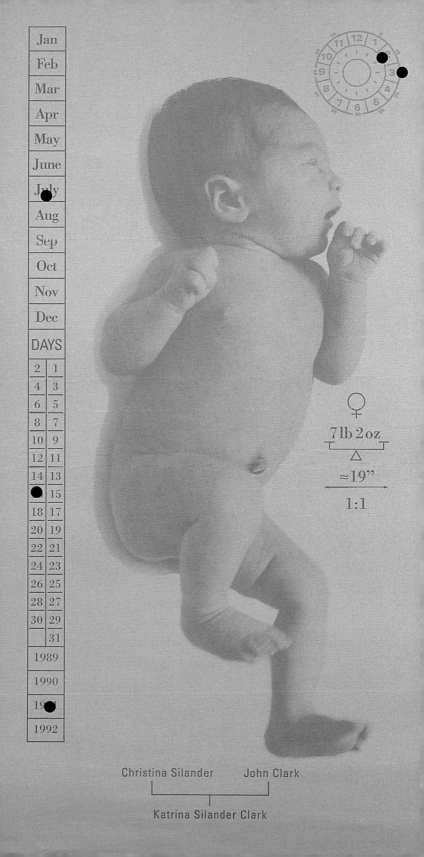

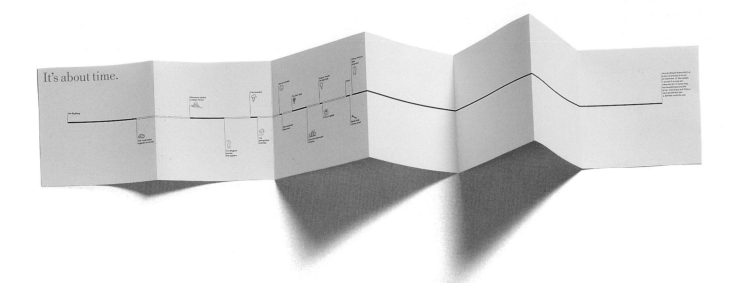

(THIS PAGE TOP) ART DIRECTORS: WILLIE BARONET, STEVE GIBBS DESIGNERS: WILLIE BARONET, META JOHNSON NEWHOUSE, KELLYE KIMBALL AGENCY: GIBBS BARONET COUNTRY: USA □ (THIS PAGE BOTTOM) ART DIRECTOR/DESIGNER: WOLFGANG HASLINGER COUNTRY: AUSTRIA □ (OPPOSITE) ART DIRECTOR/DESIGNER: ANNE MASTERS PRODUCTION COMPANIES: MCILHENNY COMPANY, DOMINO SUGAR, CAFÉ KONDITOREI SHATZ AGENCY: ANNE MASTERS DESIGN COUNTRY: USA

CATHLIN O'REILLY

PETER MÜLLER

CATHLIN O'REILLY
PETER MÜLLER

CATHLIN O'REILLY
PETER MÜLLER

CATHLIN O'REILLY
ELENA
PETER MÜLLER

Geboren am 24.März 1993 • Elena Livia Müller • Born on March 24, 1993

(LEFT) ART DIRECTOR/DESIGNER: IRENE MÜLLER COUNTRY: GERMANY □ (RIGHT) DESIGNER: ANDREA TILK COUNTRY: GERMANY □ (OPPOSITE) DESIGNER: RUEDI BAUR AGENCY: INTÉGRAL RUEDI BAUR ET ASSOCIÉS COUNTRY: FRANCE

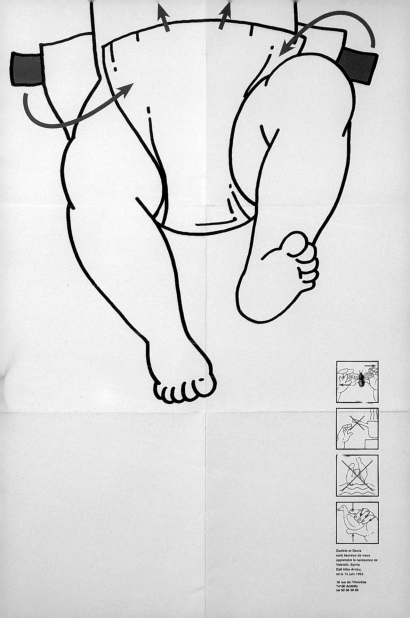

Danièle et Denis
sont heureux de vous
apprendre la naissance de
Valentin, Sylvio
Dalí Alba-Arnau,
né le 14 juin 1993.

16 rue de l'Helvétie
74100 Ambilly
tel 50 38 39 98

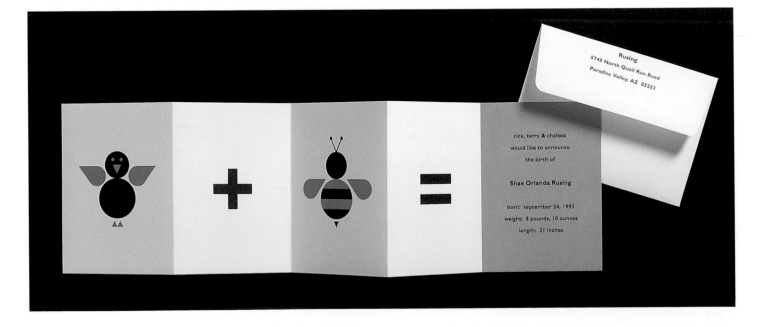

(TOP) ART DIRECTOR/DESIGNER/PHOTOGRAPHER: ALAN BROOKS COPYWRITERS: HEATHER BROOKS, ALAN BROOKS AGENCY: BROOKS CHAMPION INC. COUNTRY: USA □ (BOTTOM) ART DIRECTORS/DESIGNERS: STEVE DITKO, MIKE CAMPBELL ILLUSTRATOR: MARISSA BENINCASA AGENCY: CAMPBELL FISHER DITKO DESIGN COUNTRY: USA □ (OPPOSITE TOP) ART DIRECTOR/DESIGNER/PHOTOGRAPHER: PETER R. BITTER AGENCY: BITTER AGENTUR FÜR WERBUNG UND KOMMUNI-KATION COUNTRY: GERMANY □ (BOTTOM) ART DIRECTOR/DESIGNER/PHOTOGRAPHER: IVO VON RENNER COUNTRY: GERMANY

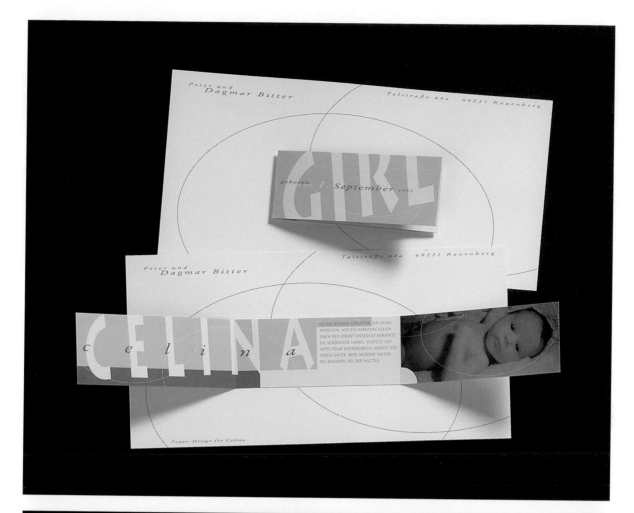

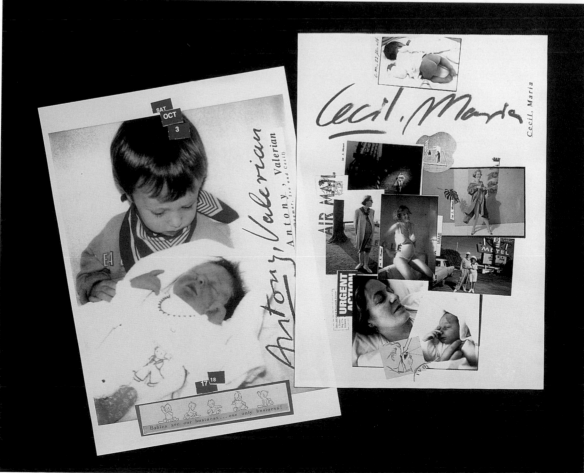

In Denmark and Sweden there is a custom of baking a Yule boar at Christmas. This custom began with the pagan belief that a benificent grain spirit existed within their crops. To embody this spirit throughout the winter, ancient Scandinavians used the flour from the last sheaf harvested to bake

a boar-shaped loaf — the boar symbolized their god of rep   g and sowing pieces of the Yule boar at spring planting, the grain spirit was returned to the crops to ensure a bountiful harvest. T   may h   n the original boaring winter. *Have a wonderful 1994.* M. Skjei Design Co.

X is for Xmas
because X is part
of the ancient
greek Chrismon,
Christ's monogram.

X referes also
to the Roman
numeral ten = X
This X is for break
into the final
decennium of the
20th century.

Merry Xmas
and a very Happy
New Year

Bruno & Ruth Wiese

Bruno & Ruth Wiese

glückliches 1990
Frohe Weihnachten
und ein sehr

Jahrhunderts.
Dezenniums dieses
des letzten
für den Anbruch
steht hier auch
X als römische Zehn

anstelle von Christmas.
So auch in 'Xmas'
Christusmonogramms.
Chrismons, des
altgriechischen
X ist Teil des

(THIS SPREAD) ART DIRECTOR: JEFF MILSTEIN DESIGNER: JEFF MILSTEIN ILLUSTRATOR: JEFF
MILSTEIN AGENCY: JEFF MILSTEIN STUDIO CLIENT: MUSEUM OF MODERN ART COUNTRY: USA

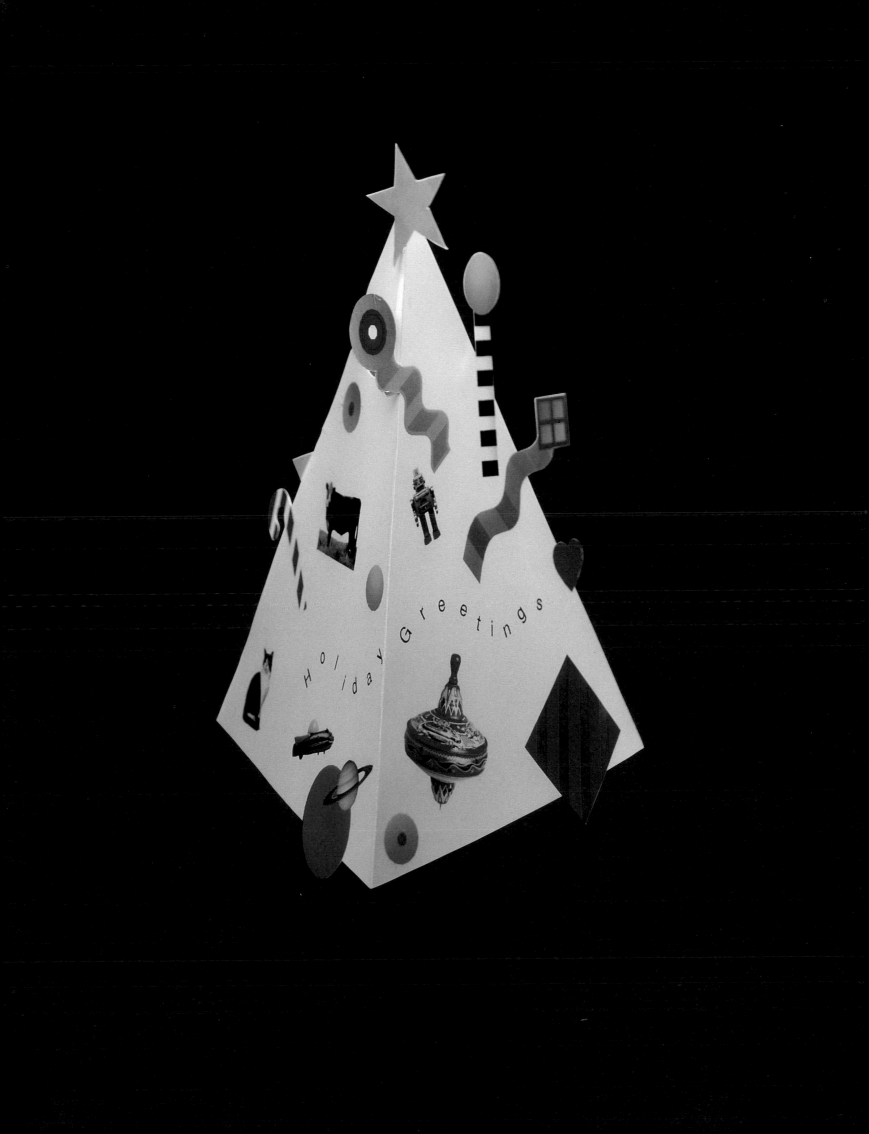

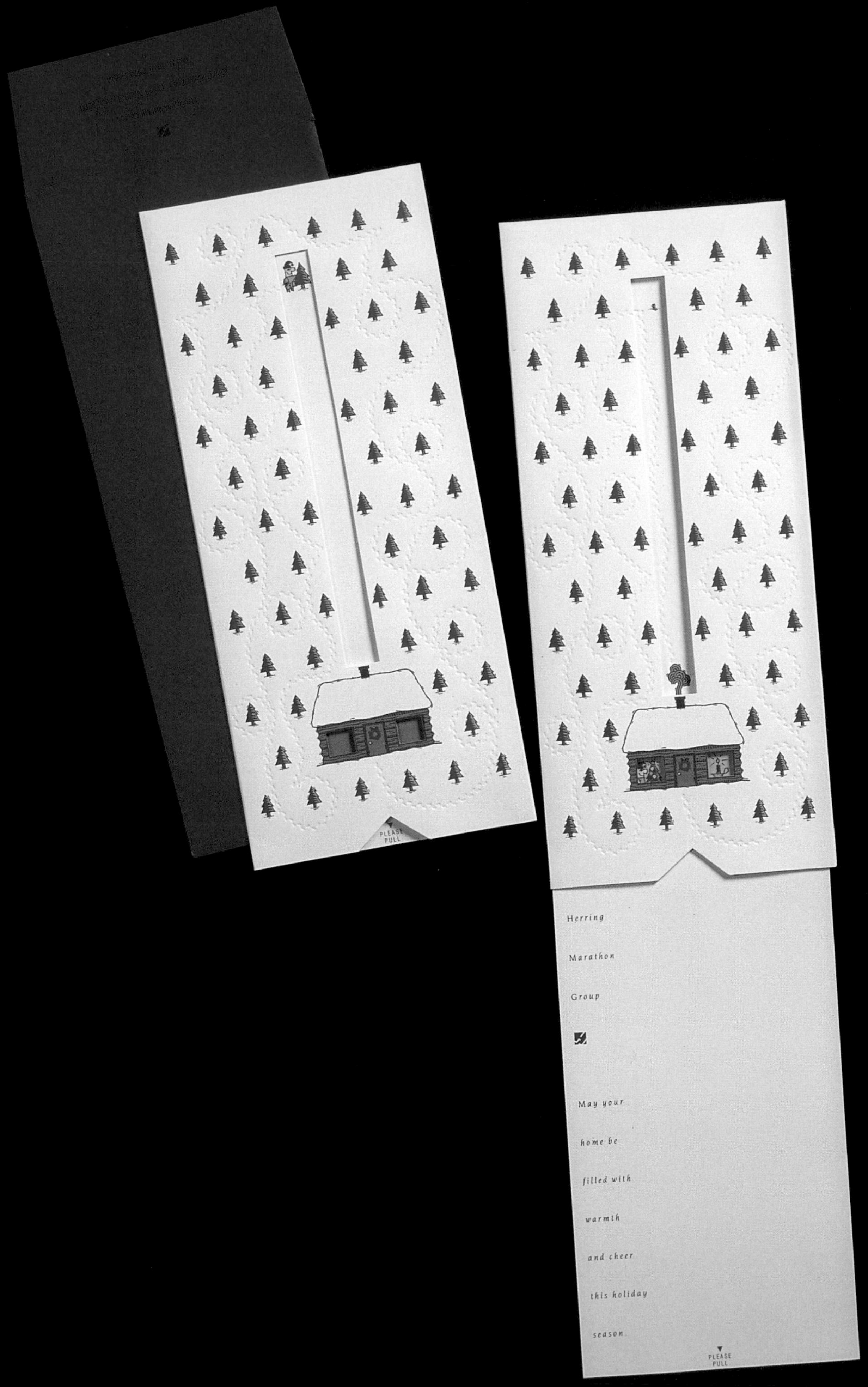

Herring

Marathon

Group

May your

home be

filled with

warmth

and cheer

this holiday

season.

PLEASE
PULL

Shiny runners whisper through the snow,

A Christmas sled, remembered, long ago.

All varnished pride and swift, it brought

The wind's cold kiss, and little sister

Waiting for her ride. The tug and struggle

Up the slope, mittens frozen to the rope.

A rush and flop—and we had wings again! Until

At last, the sun has disappeared behind the hill. Then

Home we trudged. Contented. Frozen in the fading light,

Our runnered glory set upright, outside the door,

To soar another day....

This season, which makes memory bright,

We wish you all a child's delight.

A hill that's gentle, run that's clear,

The joy of childhood through the year....

Cook and Shanosky Associates Inc.

(OPPOSITE) ART DIRECTOR/DESIGNER/COPYWRITER: BOB DENNARD ILLUSTRATOR: BRAD WINES AGENCY: DENNARD CREATIVE, INC. CLIENT: HERRING MARATHON GROUP COUNTRY: USA □ (THIS PAGE) ART DIRECTOR/DESIGNER/PHOTOGRAPHER: ROGER COOK COPYWRITER: DAVID L. EYNON AGENCY/CLIENT: COOK AND SHANOSKY ASSOCIATES, INC. COUNTRY: USA

**PACKING IS ONLY
PROTECTIVE FOR
THE ORIGINAL.**

DIE KLEINE
WEIHNACHTSFEIER.

(THIS SPREAD) ART DIRECTOR: ANDREAS BECKMANN DESIGNER: DAGMAR MÜLLER AGENCY/CLIENT: PERFACT WERBEAGENTUR COUNTRY: GERMANY

Art Director: SEYMOUR CHWAST Designer: GREG SIMPSON Photographer: SCOTT STERNBACH Agency: THE
PUSHPIN GROUP Client: BUTLER ROGERS BASKETT Country: USA □ (Opposite) Art Director/Illustrator: BRUNO
HAAG Designer: THOMAS HENSCHKE Agency/Client: BRUNO HAAG KONZEPTION & ART DIRECTION Country: GERMANY

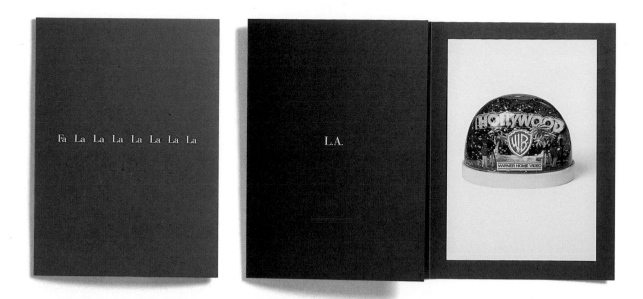

(OPPOSITE) ART DIRECTOR/DESIGNER/CLIENT: DEWITT KENDALL AGENCY: DEWITT KENDALL-CHICAGO COUNTRY: USA □ (THIS PAGE TOP) ART DIRECTOR: MICHAEL BROCK DESIGNER: MICHAEL BROCK PHOTOGRAPHER: TOM KELLER AGENCY: MICHAEL BROCK DESIGN CLIENT: WARNER HOME VIDEO COUNTRY: USA □ (BOTTOM) ART DIRECTOR: ERIC RICKA-BAUGH DESIGNER: MICHAEL SMITH ILLUSTRATOR: MICHAEL SMITH AGENCY/CLIENT: RICKABAUGH GRAPHICS COUNTRY: USA

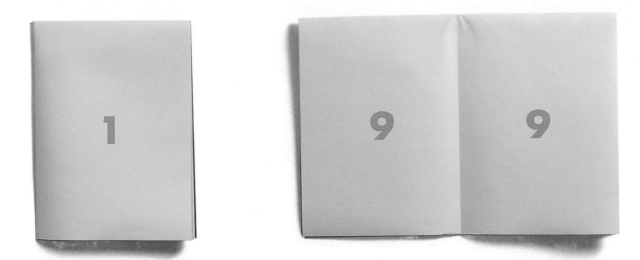

DIDIER LECOINTRE
DOMINIQUE DROUET
VOUS SOUHAITENT
UNE BONNE ANNÉE

(THIS PAGE) ART DIRECTOR: PHILIPPE GHIELMETTI DESIGNER: PHILIPPE GHIELMETTI AGENCY: SKETCH STUDIO CLIENTS:
DIDIER LECOINTRE, DENIS OZANNE COUNTRY: FRANCE □ (OPPOSITE PAGE) ART DIRECTOR: DAVID LERCH
DESIGNER/ILLUSTRATOR: DAVID LERCH COPYWRITER: LISA LERCH AGENCY/CLIENT: PENNEBAKER DESIGN COUNTRY: USA

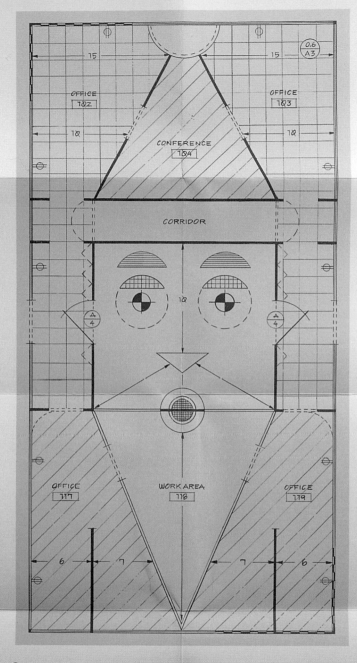

may the peace of this joyous season

carry you through the new year

michael brock design

nie mehr treiben

weiße weihnacht

schwarze

weste

immer

vierundneunzig klappt es

nie mehr schwarz sehen

schwarze zahlen

immer grün

vierundneunzig klappt es

ein buntes treiben

weiße weihnacht

weiße weste

ndneunzig klappt es

(THIS PAGE TOP) ART DIRECTOR/DESIGNER: LYNDA BROCKBANK AGENCY/CLIENT: CRESCENT LODGE DESIGN COUNTRY: GREAT
BRITAIN □ (THIS PAGE BOTTOM) ART DIRECTOR: DAVID CARTER DESIGNER: RANDALL HILL PHOTOGRAPHER: KLEIN
+ WILSON COPYWRITER: MARSHA COBURN AGENCY/CLIENT: DAVID CARTER GRAPHIC DESIGN ASSOCIATES COUNTRY: USA

Wolfgang Haslinger, 3400 Klosterneuburg, Hölzlgasse 15/15

Sabine Koch
3400 Klbg,
Hölzlg. 15/15

den hatte,
tauchte er auf,
hockte sich an
den Brunnen-
rand und spitzte
hoffnungsvoll

sein breites Maul
zum Kuß. Doch
die Prinzessin
griff sich ge-
schwind ihr
Lieblingsspiel-

(ABOVE) ART DIRECTOR/DESIGNER: WOLFGANG HASLINGER COUNTRY: AUSTRIA ☐ (OPPOSITE) ART DIRECTORS: KARI PALMQVIST,

JEANETTE PALMQVIST DESIGNER/ILLUSTRATOR: KARI PALMQVIST AGENCY/CLIENT: BUBBLAN STUDIO COUNTRY: SWEDEN

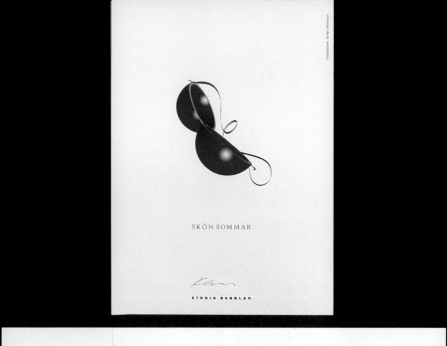

SKÖN SOMMAR

STUDIO BUBBLAN

GOD JUL

GOTT NYTT ÅR

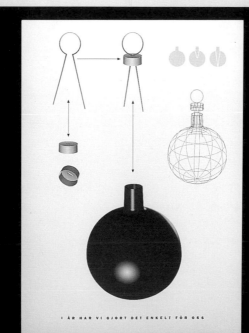

I ÅR HAR VI GJORT DET ENKELT FÖR OSS

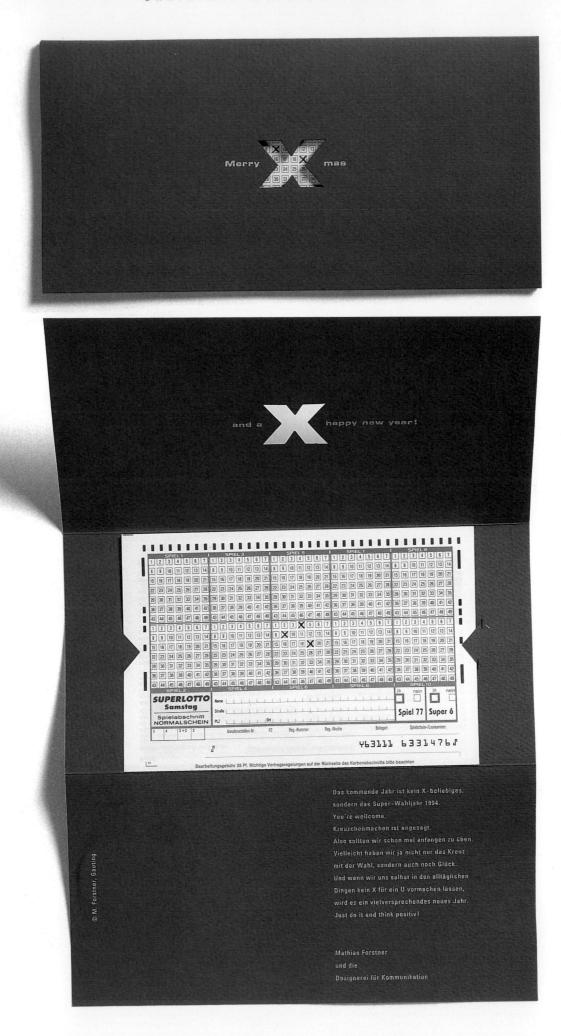

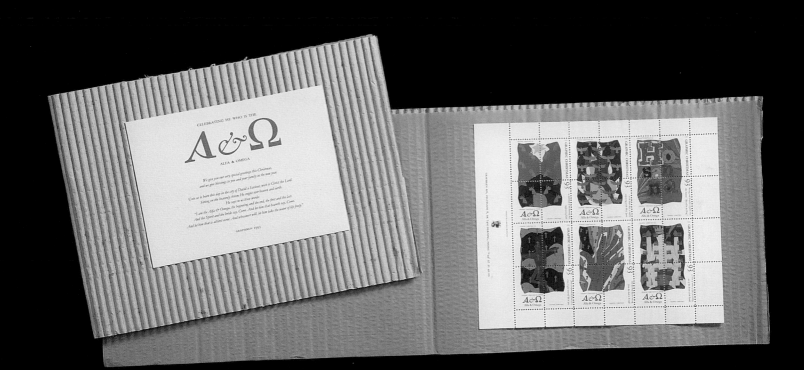

(OPPOSITE) ART DIRECTOR/DESIGNER: MATHIAS FORSTNER AGENCY/CLIENT: DESIGNEREI F. KOMMUNIKATION COUNTRY: GERMANY □ (THIS PAGE TOP) ART DIRECTOR/DESIGNER/ILLUSTRATOR: CARSTEN SKOVLUND AGENCY/CLIENT: GRAFIKKEN COUNTRY: DENMARK □ (THIS PAGE BOTTOM LEFT) ART DIRECTOR: GARRY EMERY DESIGNER/AGENCY/ CLIENT: EMERY VINCENT ASSOCIATES COUNTRY: AUSTRALIA □ (THIS PAGE BOTTOM RIGHT) ART DIRECTOR/DESIGNER/ PHOTOGRAPHER/ILLUSTRATOR: KENNETH KARLSSON AGENCY/CLIENT: ATELJÉ ELEFANTEN & FARET AB COUNTRY: SWEDEN

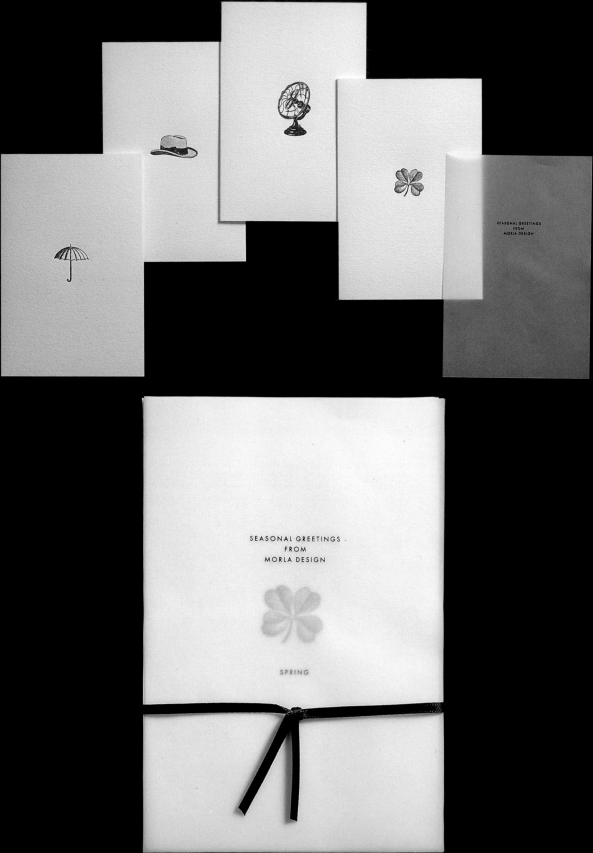

(Opposite) ART DIRECTOR: JENNIFER MORLA DESIGNERS: JENNIFER MORLA, CRAIG BAILEY AGENCY/CLIENT: MORLA DESIGN COUNTRY: USA □ (ABOVE) ART DIRECTOR/DESIGNER: R.O. BLECHMAN AGENCY: R.O. BLECHMAN, INC. CLIENT: THE INK TANK COUNTRY: USA

(THIS PAGE TOP) ART DIRECTOR/DESIGNER: MICHAEL BROCK PHOTOGRAPHER: TOM KELLER AGENCY/CLIENT: MICHAEL BROCK
DESIGN COUNTRY: USA □ (THIS PAGE BOTTOM) ART DIRECTOR: PIER PAOLO PITALLO ILLUSTRATOR: PAOLO D'ALTAN
AGENCY: CENTO PER CENTO COUNTRY: ITALY □ (OPPOSITE PAGE) ART DIRECTORS: BOB HAMBLY, BARBARA
WOOLLEY DESIGNERS: BOB HAMBLY, BARBARA WOOLLEY AGENCY/CLIENT: HAMBLY & WOOLLEY INC. COUNTRY: CANADA

MARIA CRISTINA ROMAGNOLI GRAFICA VIA MASSACIUCCOLI 12 00199 ROMA TEL 06/ 86.21.82.60

(OPPOSITE PAGE) ART DIRECTOR: ROLAND SCHNEIDER DESIGNER: MICHAELA BAUER AGENCY: BAUERS BÜRO CLIENT: FASHION STAGE COUNTRY: GERMANY ◻ (ABOVE) ART DIRECTOR/DESIGNER/CLIENT: MARIA CRISTINA ROMAGNOLI COUNTRY: ITALY

(THIS PAGE TOP) ART DIRECTOR: JULIA CHONG TAM DESIGNER: JULIA CHONG TAM ILLUSTRATOR: JULIA CHONG TAM AGENCY/CLIENT: JULIA TAM DESIGN COUNTRY: USA □ (THIS PAGE BOTTOM) ART DIRECTORS: LYNN TRICKETT, BRIAN WEBB DESIGNERS: LYNN TRICKETT, BRIAN WEBB, ANDREW THOMAS ILLUSTRATORS/STUDIO/CLIENT: TRICKETT & WEBB LIMITED COUNTRY: GREAT BRITAIN □ (OPPOSITE PAGE) ART DIRECTOR: BYRON JACOBS DESIGNERS: BYRON JACOBS, MICHELLE SHEK ILLUSTRATOR: PPA DESIGN LIMITED AGENCY/CLIENT: PPA DESIGN LIMITED COUNTRY: HONG KONG

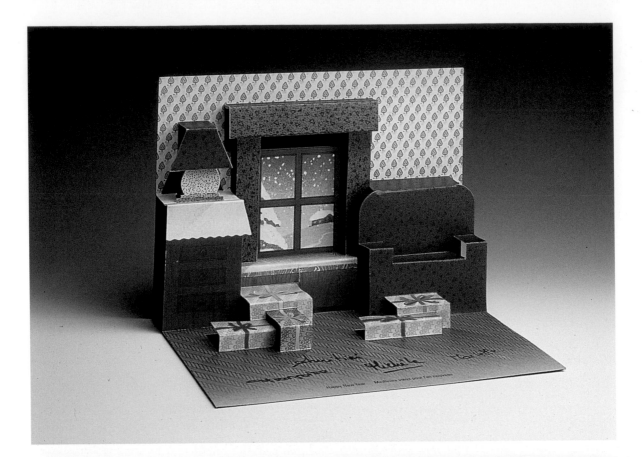

(THIS PAGE TOP) ART DIRECTOR/DESIGNER: EDUARD CEHOVIN PHOTOGRAPHER: BORIS GABERSCEK AGENCY: M DESIGN CLIENT: EBEL MONTRES SA COUNTRY: SWITZERLAND □ (THIS PAGE BOTTOM) ART DIRECTOR/DESIGNER/ILLUSTRATOR: WOLFGANG HASLINGER CLIENT: SOLID AUDIO COUNTRY: AUSTRIA □ (OPPOSITE PAGE) ART DIRECTORS/DESIGNERS: JEFF LARSON, SCOTT JOHNSON COPYWRITER: JEFF LARSON AGENCY/CLIENT: LARSON DESIGN ASSOCIATES COUNTRY: USA

(THIS PAGE TOP) ART DIRECTOR: JOSE SERRANO DESIGNER: JOSE SERRANO ILLUSTRATOR: MIRES DESIGN STAFF AGENCY:

MIRES DESIGN CLIENT: MIRES DESIGN COUNTRY: USA ▫ (THIS PAGE CENTER AND BOTTOM) ART DIRECTOR/DESIGNER:

JULIA CHONG TAM ILLUSTRATOR: JULIA CHONG TAM AGENCY/CLIENT: JULIA TAM DESIGN COUNTRY: USA ▫

(OPPOSITE TOP LEFT) ART DIRECTORS: LO BREIER, ANDREAS MIEDANER DESIGNER: CARL VAN OMMEN AGENCY/CLIENT: BÜRO X

DIE FESTSTELLBREMSE FÜR
DIE WEIHNACHTSAUTOMATIK
WIRD MIT HILFE DER NEU-
JAHRSRUTSCHKUPPLUNG AM
WUNSCHBAROMETER JUSTIERT.

Oehsler '93

295/300

Handcolorierter Druck von Uwe Ochsler in einer Auflage von dreihun-
dert Stück. Eine Serie von dreißig kleinformatigen Original-Zeichnun-
gen (90x130 mm) dieser Art wird vom 4. Dezember 1993 bis Ende des
Jahres in der Kölner Galerie „Kunstraum am Buttermarkt" ausgestellt.

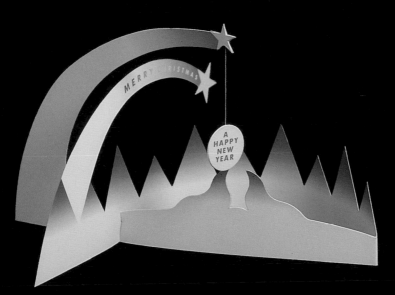

GERMANY □ (THIS PAGE TOP RIGHT) ART DIRECTOR: JOHN PARHAM DESIGNER/ILLUSTRATOR: MARUCHI SANTANA
AGENCY/CLIENT: PARHAM SANTANA DESIGN COUNTRY: USA □ (THIS PAGE CENTER) ART DIRECTOR: BARBARA
BORGSTÄDT DESIGNER/AGENCY: BARBARA BORGSTÄDT ILLUSTRATOR: UWE OCHSLER COUNTRY: GERMANY □ (THIS

GIFTWRAP

GIFTWRAP

PRIMO ANGELI

NO. OF 700 SETS

NO. OF 700 SETS

(OPPOSITE PAGE) ART DIRECTOR/DESIGNER: PRIMO ANGELI CLIENT: PRIMO ANGELI INC. COUNTRY: USA □ (THIS PAGE) ART
DIRECTORS: MIKE HICKS, TOM POTH DESIGNERS: MIKE HICKS, MATT HECK AGENCY/CLIENT: HIXO, INC. COUNTRY: USA

(THIS PAGE TOP) ART DIRECTORS/DESIGNERS/CLIENTS: MARTINA EISELEIN, HEIKE SCHIRMER PHOTOGRAPHER: DIETMAR HORNUNG COUNTRY: GERMANY □ (THIS PAGE BOTTOM) ART DIRECTOR/DESIGNER: KEISUKE UNOSAWA AGENCY/CLIENT: KEISUKE UNOSAWA DESIGN COUNTRY: JAPAN □ (OPPOSITE) ART DIRECTOR/DESIGNER/CLIENT: DAVID TARTAKOVER AGENCY: TARTAKOVER DESIGN COUNTRY: ISRAEL □ (FOLLOWING SPREAD LEFT) DESIGNERS: TODD WATERBURY, SHARON WERNER CONSTRUCTION DESIGNER: BERNIE LECLERC ILLUSTRATORS: LYNN SCHULTE, TODD WATERBURY, SHARON WERNER AGENCY/CLIENT: DUFFY, INC. COUNTRY: USA □ (FOLLOWING SPREAD RIGHT) ART DIRECTOR: GARRY EMERY DESIGNER/AGENCY: EMERY VINCENT ASSOCIATES CLIENT: CARMEN FURNITURE (SALES) PTY LTD. COUNTRY: AUSTRALIA

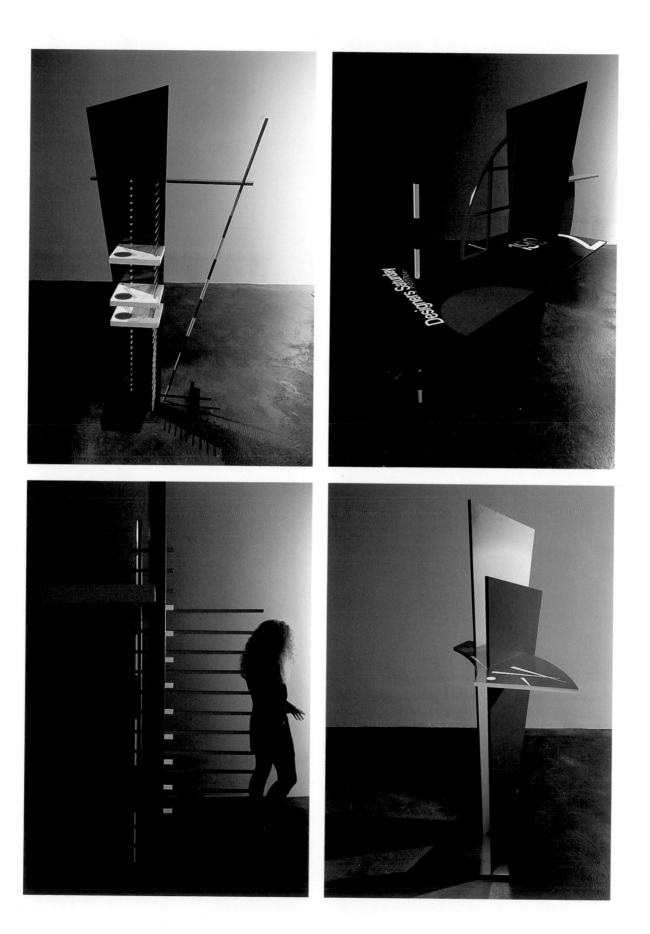

(OPPOSITE) ART DIRECTOR: CHARLES S. ANDERSON DESIGNERS: CHARLES S. ANDERSON, TODD HAUSWIRTH PHOTOGRAPHER: DARRELL
EAGER ILLUSTRATOR: CSA ARCHIVE AGENCY/CLIENT: CHARLES S. ANDERSON DESIGN CO. COUNTRY: USA □ (THIS PAGE
TOP) ART DIRECTOR/DESIGNER: BARRIE TUCKER AGENCY/CLIENT: TUCKER DESIGN COUNTRY: AUSTRALIA □ (BOTTOM) ART
DIRECTOR/DESIGNER: CLIVE H. GAY PHOTOGRAPHER: ROLAND MEISSNER AGENCY/CLIENT: TRADEMARK DESIGN COUNTRY: SOUTH AFRICA

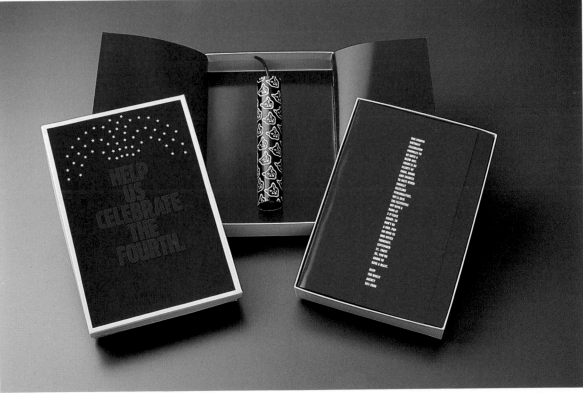

(TOP) ART DIRECTOR/DESIGNER: MONIKA UHLMANN PHOTOGRAPHERS: FOTOSTUDIO KONRAD HOFFMANN, COSMO-TONE (BACKGROUND) CLIENT: UHLMANN GRAPHICDESIGNERS COUNTRY: GERMANY □ (BOTTOM) ART DIRECTOR/ DESIGNER: CHARLES HIVELY AGENCY/CLIENT: THE HIVELY AGENCY, INC. COUNTRY: USA □ (OPPOSITE) ART DIRECTOR/DESIGNER: SHARON WERNER AGENCY: DUFFY, INC. CLIENT: FOX RIVER PAPER COMPANY COUNTRY: USA

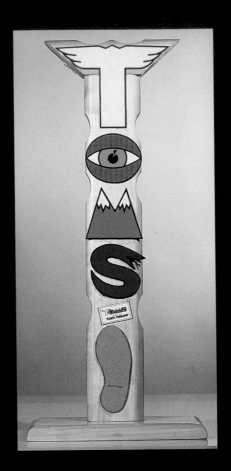

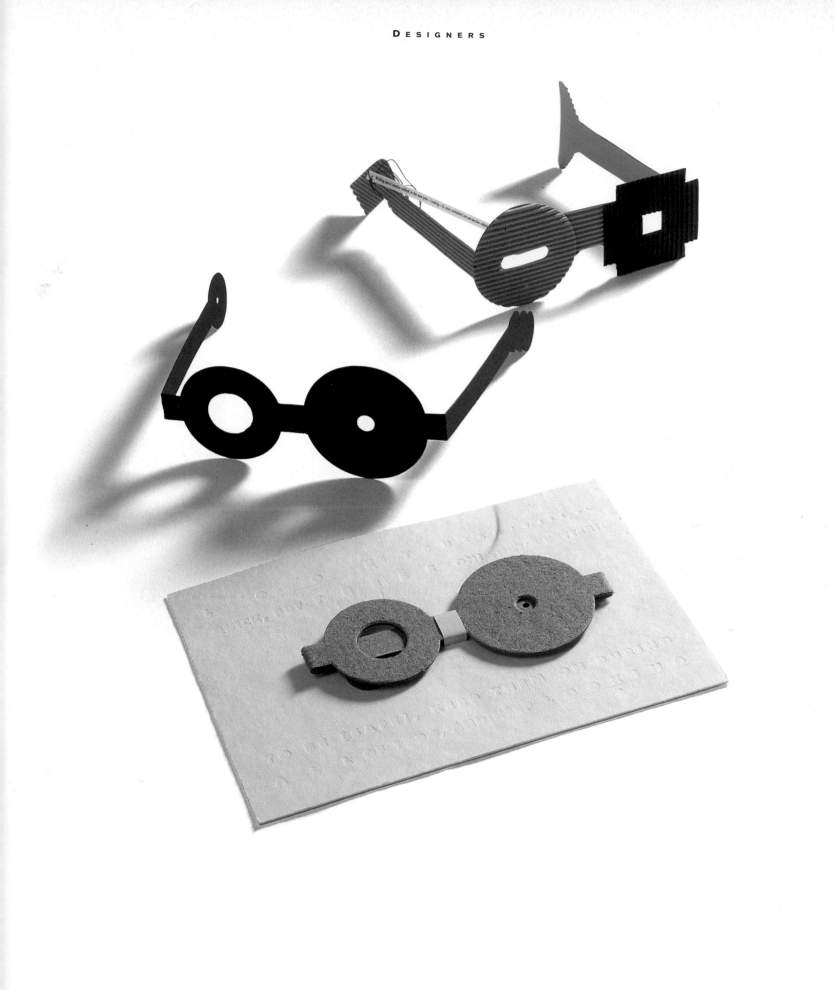

(OPPOSITE TOP) ART DIRECTORS: CORNELIA STOFFREGEN, JOSEF SCHEWE PHOTOGRAPHER: FRIEDRUN REINHOLD AGENCY: DIE WERBEAGENTUR FFF CLIENT: TERRANO SCHUH GMBH COUNTRY: GERMANY □ (BOTTOM) ART DIRECTOR: KEISUKE UNOSAWA DESIGNER: KEISUKE UNOSAWA AGENCY: KEISUKE UNOSAWA DESIGN CLIENT: KEISUKE UNOSAWA DESIGN COUNTRY: JAPAN □ (ABOVE) ART DIRECTOR: JOHN CLARK DESIGNER: JOHN CLARK AGENCY/CLIENT: LOOKING COUNTRY: USA

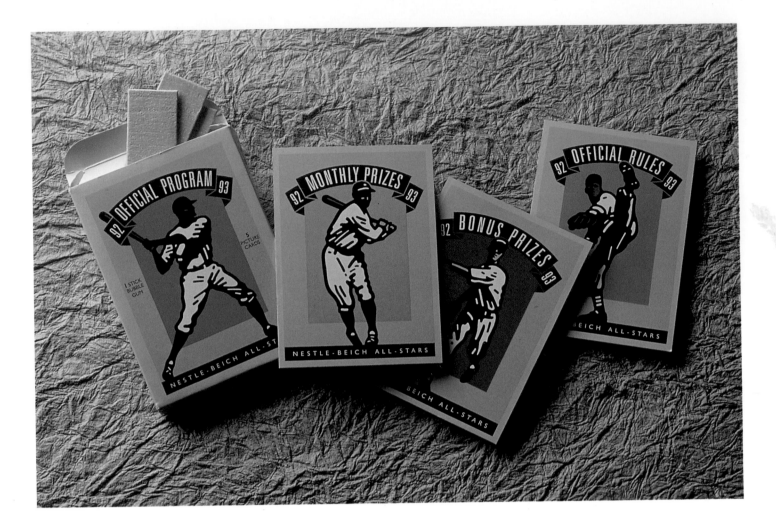

(THIS PAGE) **1** ART DIRECTOR/DESIGNER: BRUCE EDWARDS ILLUSTRATOR: MICHAEL SCHWAB AGENCY: RAPP COLLINS COMMUNI-CATIONS CLIENT: KATHRYN BEICH (NESTLE-BEICH'S FUNDRAISING) COUNTRY: USA □ (OPPOSITE, FROM TOP LEFT TO BOTTOM RIGHT) **2, 5** ART DIRECTOR: CHARLES S. ANDERSON DESIGNERS: CHARLES S. ANDERSON, DANIEL OLSON PHOTOGRAPHER: PAUL IRMITER AGENCY/CLIENT: CHARLES S. ANDERSON DESIGN CO. COUNTRY: USA □ **3** ART DIRECTOR/DESIGNER: JOSE SERRANO PHOTOGRAPHER: CARL VANDERSCHUIT ILLUSTRATOR: TRACY SABIN AGENCY: MIRES DESIGN, INC. CLIENT: BORDEAUX PRINTERS COUNTRY: USA □ **4** ART DIRECTOR/DESIGNER: BARRY A. MERTEN PHOTOGRAPHER: DOUG STEWART AGENCY: MERTEN DESIGN GROUP CLIENT: MERTEN DESIGN GROUP COUNTRY: USA

(THIS PAGE) ART DIRECTOR: CAROL HOOVER DESIGNERS: CAROL HOOVER, MICHAEL HINSHAW AGENCY/CLIENT: TRIAD, INC.

COUNTRY: USA □ (OPPOSITE PAGE) ART DIRECTOR: THOMAS OTTE DESIGNER: INES KASPER COPYWRITER: CLAUDIA

LANDWEHR AGENCY: STIEHL/OTTE WERBEAGENTUR GMBH CLIENT: STIEHL/OTTE WERBEAGENTUR GMBH COUNTRY: GERMANY

LIEBER HERR SCHNEIDEWIND!

WENN SIE EINMAL
MIT IHRER AGENTUR
LIEGENBLEIBEN,
IST ES GUT, EINE
RESERVE ZU HABEN,
DIE SIE WIEDER
VORANBRINGT.

VIELLEICHT SOGAR BIS OSNABRÜCK.
STIEHL / OTTE

(THIS PAGE) ART DIRECTORS: ROBYNNE RAYE, VITTORIO COSTARELLA DESIGNERS: ROBYNNE RAYE, VITTORIO COSTARELLA, MICHAEL STRASSBURGER AGENCY/CLIENT: MODERN DOG COUNTRY: USA □ (OPPOSITE, FROM TOP LEFT TO BOTTOM RIGHT) 1 ART DIRECTOR/DESIGNER: THOMAS G. FOWLER AGENCY: TOM FOWLER, INC. CLIENT: GRAPHICS 3 COUNTRY: USA □ 2 ART DIRECTOR/DESIGNER: KAREN MURRAY AGENCY/CLIENT: DESIGNWORKS COUNTRY: NEW ZEALAND □ 3 ART DIRECTOR/DESIGNER: WOLFGANG HASLINGER COUNTRY: AUSTRIA □ 4 ART DIRECTOR: HUGO PUTTAERT DESIGNERS: HUGO PUTTAERT, JOHAN JACOBS, POL QUADENS AGENCY/CLIENT: VISION & FACTORY COUNTRY: BELGIUM □ 5 DESIGNERS: FRANCISCO RIOS, JIM MOUSNER AGENCY/CLIENT: TRIBE! DESIGN COUNTRY: USA □ 6 ART DIRECTION: (Z)OO PRODUKTIES, ANITA STEKETEE DESIGNERS/ILLUSTRATORS: VARIOUS AGENCY/CLIENT: (Z)OO PRODUKTIES, ERIC VAN CASTEREN, ROBERT VAN RIXTEL COUNTRY: NETHERLANDS □ 7 ART DIRECTOR/ DESIGNER: GRANT JORGENSEN COPYWRITER: ROGER LIMINTON AGENCY: GRANT JORGENSEN DESIGN CLIENT: LIMINTON CORCORAN DESIGN COUNTRY: AUSTRALIA □ 8 ART DIRECTOR/DESIGNER: WOLFGANG HASLINGER COUNTRY: AUSTRIA □ (FOLLOWING SPREAD LEFT) ART DIRECTORS: STEVE WEDEEN, RICK VAUGHN, DANIEL MICHAEL FLYNN DESIGNER: DANIEL MICHAEL FLYNN ILLUSTRATOR: BILL GERHOLD AGENCY/CLIENT: VAUGHN WEDEEN CREATIVE COUNTRY: USA □ (FOLLOWING SPREAD RIGHT) ART DIRECTOR: BARRIE TUCKER DESIGNERS: BARRIE TUCKER, HANS KOHLA AGENCY: TUCKER DESIGN CLIENT: WOODS BAGOT COUNTRY: AUSTRALIA

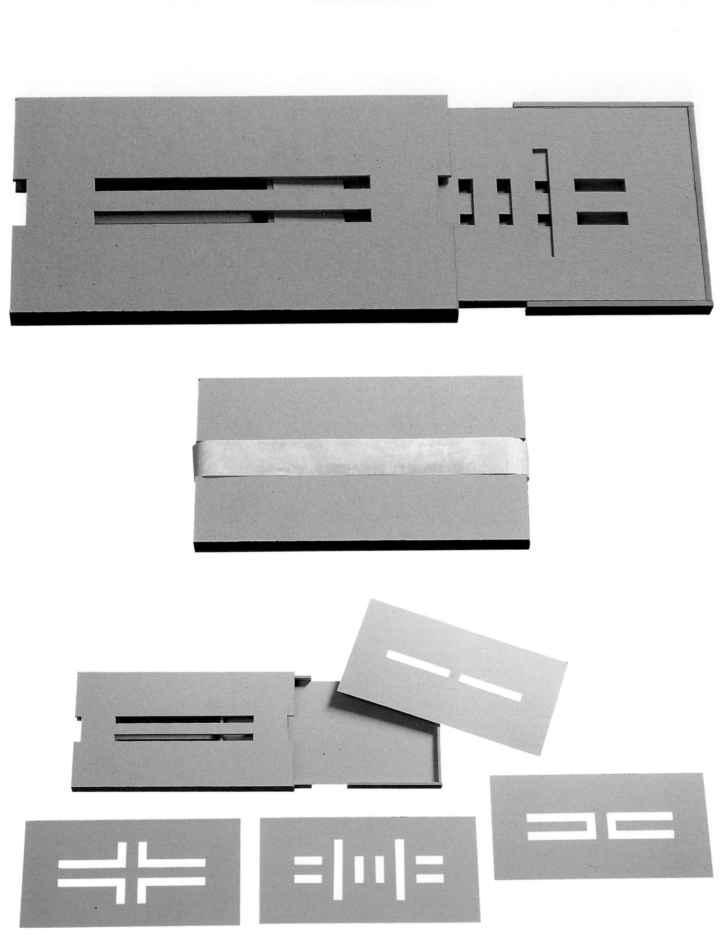

(OPPOSITE) ART DIRECTOR/DESIGNER/AGENCY/CLIENT: RALF STUTZ COUNTRY: GERMANY □ (ABOVE, TOP LEFT) ART DIRECTOR: RICK VAUGHN DESIGNER/ILLUSTRATOR: DANIEL MICHAEL FLYNN AGENCY/CLIENT: VAUGHN WEDEEN CREATIVE COUNTRY: USA □ (BOTTOM LEFT) ART DIRECTOR: URS J. KNOBEL DESIGNER: KARIN BIRCHLER AGENCY: URS J. KNOBEL WERBUNG CLIENT: VICTORIA WERKE AG, MÖBELFABRIK COUNTRY: SWITZERLAND □ (CENTER) ART DIRECTOR/ DESIGNER: BARRIE TUCKER AGENCY: TUCKER DESIGN CLIENT: AVON GRAPHICS COUNTRY: AUSTRALIA □ (TOP RIGHT) ART DIRECTOR/DESIGNER: CHUCK ANDERSON ILLUSTRATOR: LYNN SCHULTE AGENCY/CLIENT: DUFFY, INC. COUNTRY: USA □ (BOTTOM RIGHT) ART DIRECTOR/DESIGNER: KURT MEINECKE AGENCY/CLIENT: GROUP/CHICAGO, INC. COUNTRY: USA

(THIS PAGE LEFT) ART DIRECTOR: CHARLES S. ANDERSON DESIGNERS: CHARLES S. ANDERSON, TODD HAUSWIRTH PHOTOGRAPHER: DARRELL EAGER AGENCY: CHARLES S. ANDERSON DESIGN CO. CLIENT: PRINT CRAFT, INC. COUNTRY: USA □ (THIS PAGE RIGHT) ART DIRECTOR: CHARLES S. ANDERSON DESIGNERS: CHARLES S. ANDERSON, TODD HAUSWIRTH PHOTOGRAPHER: PAUL IRMITER ILLUSTRATOR: CSA ARCHIVE AGENCY: CHARLES S. ANDERSON DESIGN CO. CLIENT: FRENCH PAPER CO. COUNTRY: USA □ (OPPOSITE) ART DIRECTOR/DESIGNER: CARTER WEITZ WRITER: MITCH KOCH AGENCY: BAILEY LAUERMAN & ASSOCIATES CLIENT: WESTERN PAPER COMPANY COUNTRY: USA

(Above) ART DIRECTORS: MARK CANTOR, JOEL FULLER DESIGNER: MARK CANTOR AGENCY: PINKHAUS DESIGN CLIENT: ALAN FRIED-
MAN/2424 BUILDING COUNTRY: USA □ (Opposite) CREATIVE DIRECTORS: DAVID YOUNG, JEFF LARAMORE ART DIRECTOR:
MARK BRADLEY COPYWRITER: DAVID YOUNG AGENCY: YOUNG & LARAMORE CLIENT: WILHELM CONSTRUCTION COUNTRY: USA

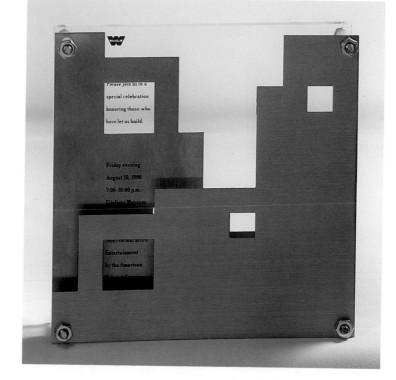

(TOP) ART DIRECTORS: MICHAEL MCGINN, TAKAAKI MATSUMOTO DESIGNER: MICHAEL MCGINN AGENCY: M PLUS M INCORPORATED CLIENT: INDEPENDENT CURATORS INCORPORATED COUNTRY: USA

□ (BOTTOM) ART DIRECTOR/DESIGNER: FONS M. HICKMANN CLIENT: GUAREDISCH I. COUNTRY: GERMANY

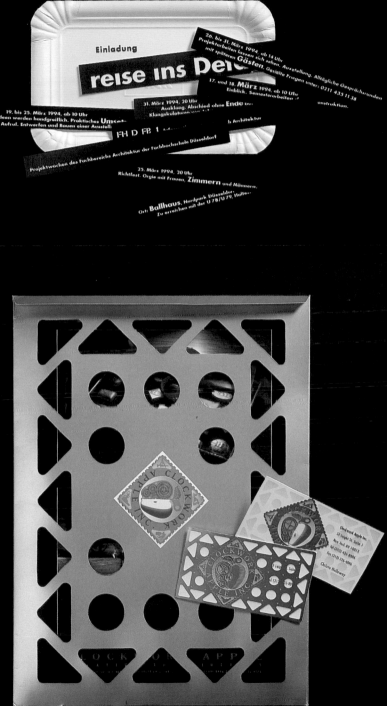

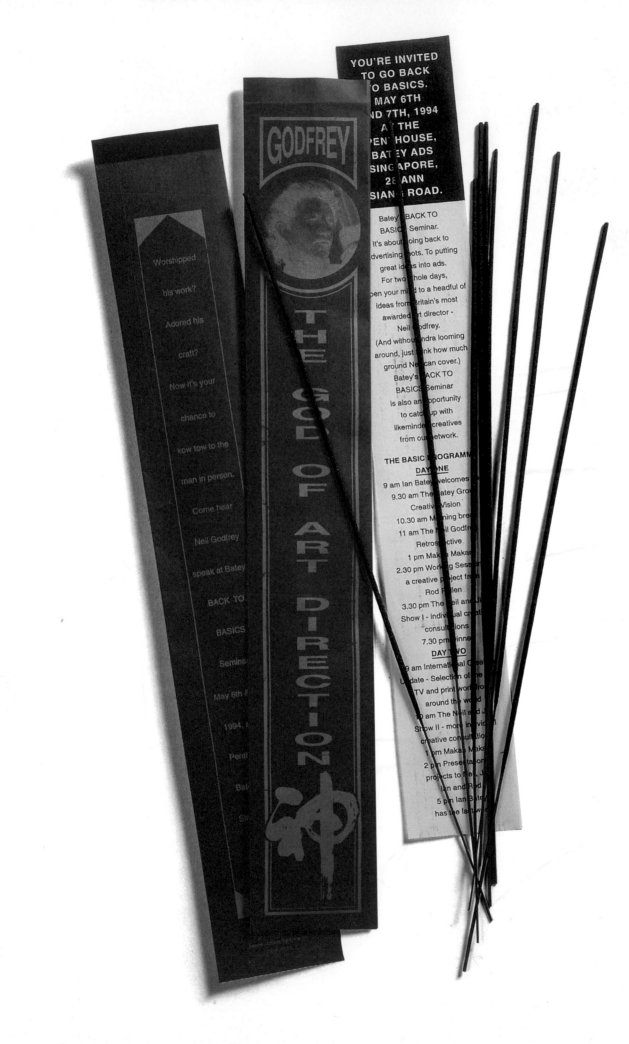

YOU'RE INVITED
TO GO BACK
TO BASICS.
MAY 6TH
AND 7TH, 1994
AT THE
PENTHOUSE,
BATEY ADS
SINGAPORE,
28 ANN
SIANG ROAD.

Batey's BACK TO
BASICS Seminar.
It's about going back to
advertising roots. To putting
great ideas into ads.
For two whole days,
open your mind to a headful of
ideas from Britain's most
awarded art director -
Neil Godfrey.
(And without Indra looming
around, just think how much
ground we can cover.)
Batey's BACK TO
BASICS Seminar
is also an opportunity
to catch up with
likeminded creatives
from our network.

THE BASIC PROGRAMME
DAY ONE
9 am Ian Batey welcomes
9.30 am The Batey Group
Creative Vision
10.30 am Morning break
11 am The Neil Godfrey
Retrospective
1 pm Makan Makan
2.30 pm Working Session -
a creative project from
Rod Pullen
3.30 pm The Neil and Jim
Show I - individual creative
consultations
7.30 pm Dinner
DAY TWO
9 am International Creative
Update - Selection of the best
TV and print work from
around the world
10 am The Neil and Jim
Show II - more individual
creative consultations
1 pm Makan Makan
2 pm Presentation of
projects to Neil, Jim,
Ian and Rod
5 pm Ian Batey
has the last word

GODFREY

THE GOD OF ART DIRECTION

神

Worshipped

his work?

Adored his

craft?

Now it's your

chance to

kow tow to the

man in person.

Come hear

Neil Godfrey

speak at Batey

BACK TO

BASICS

Seminar

May 6th &

1994, P

Penth

Bat

Sin

PHILIPPE LUIGGI / LIBRAIRIE DENISE WEIL
DIDIER LECOINTRE - DENIS OZANNE

RELIURES
LETTRISTES

AMARGER BROUTIN CANAL CARAVEN
DEVAUX DUPONT HACHETTE
DELATOUR LEMAÎTRE ISOU LETAILLEUR
LEONCINI MULLER POYET RICHOL
ROEHMER SABATIER SATIÉ SPACAGNA

VERNISSAGE

LE JEUDI 21 MARS 1991 A 18 HEURES
A LA LIBRAIRIE LECOINTRE-OZANNE
9, RUE DE TOURNON PARIS 6ème
TEL (1) 43 26 02 92

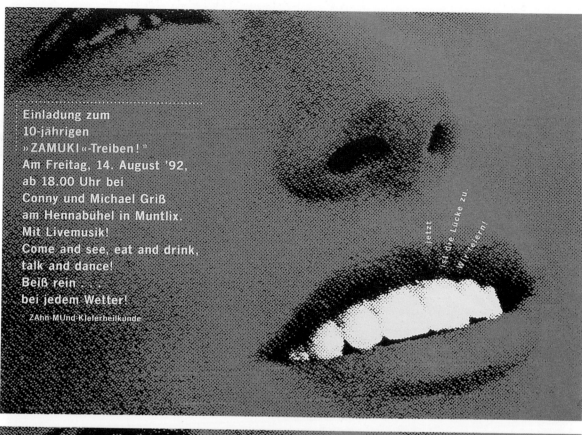

Einladung zum
10-jährigen
»ZAMUKI«-Treiben!*
Am Freitag, 14. August '92,
ab 18.00 Uhr bei
Conny und Michael Griß
am Hennabühel in Muntlix.
Mit Livemusik!
Come and see, eat and drink,
talk and dance!
Beiß rein . . .
bei jedem Wetter!
* ZAhn-MUnd-Kieferheilkunde

Jetzt
ist die Lücke zu.
Wir feiern!

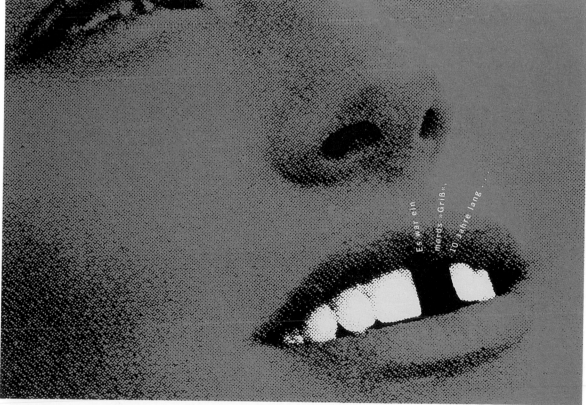

Es war ein
mords-»Griß«,
10 Jahre lang . . .

(OPPOSITE) ART DIRECTOR/DESIGNER/ILLUSTRATOR: THOMAS G. FOWLER AGENCY/CLIENT: TOM FOWLER, INC. COUNTRY: USA □ (THIS PAGE) ART DIRECTOR/DESIGNER: PETER FELDER AGENCY: FELDER GRAFIK DESIGN CLIENT: DR. MICHAEL GRISS COUNTRY: AUSTRIA

2 . A U T O R E N - R E A D E R

MICHAEL KLAUS

JOHN LINTHICUM

HELGA LIPPELT

INGE MEYER-DIETRICH

CLAUDIA PÜTZ

JUTTA RICHTER

SCHREIBEN LESEN HÖREN

LINDE ROTTA

DIETMAR SOUS

HALIT ÜNAL

NAMEN REZENSIONEN WERKE

(OPPOSITE) ART DIRECTOR/DESIGNER: LUTZ MENZE PHOTOGRAPHER: CICO HEUKAMP AGENCY: LUTZ MENZE DESIGN CLIENT: SEKRETARIAT FÜR GEMEINSAME KULTURARBEIT IN NRW COUNTRY: GERMANY □ (THIS PAGE TOP) CREATIVE DIRECTORS: KENT HUNTER, DANNY ABELSON DESIGNERS: STEVEN FABRIZIO, GINA STONE PHOTOGRAPHER: HANS NELEMAN AND STOCK AGENCY: FRANKFURT BALKIND PARTNERS CLIENT: AMERICAN MOVIE CLASSICS COUNTRY: USA □ (BOTTOM) ART DIRECTOR/DESIGNER: SARA ROTMAN CLIENT: SONY MUSIC ENTERTAINMENT INC. COUNTRY: USA

FROM
CHANT
TO
GRANT

GET THE WHOLE PICTURE INSIDE.

MINNESOTA PUBLIC RADIO
PRESENTS

MUSIC
of the
SPIRIT

A CELEBRATION IN INSPIRATIONAL MUSIC
FROM GREGORIAN CHANT TO AMY GRANT
SUNDAY, MAY 8, 1994

(OPPOSITE) ART DIRECTORS: STEVEN SIKORA, LYNETTE ERICKSON-SIKORA DESIGNERS: BRUCE MACINDOE, STEVEN SIKORA AGENCY: DESIGN GUYS CLIENT: MINNESOTA PUBLIC RADIO COUNTRY: USA □ (THIS PAGE) ART DIRECTOR: JOHN MULLER DESIGNER: SAL COSTELL PHOTOGRAPHER: STEVE CURTIS AGENCY: MULLER + COMPANY CLIENT: KANSAS CITY ART INSTITUTE COUNTRY: USA

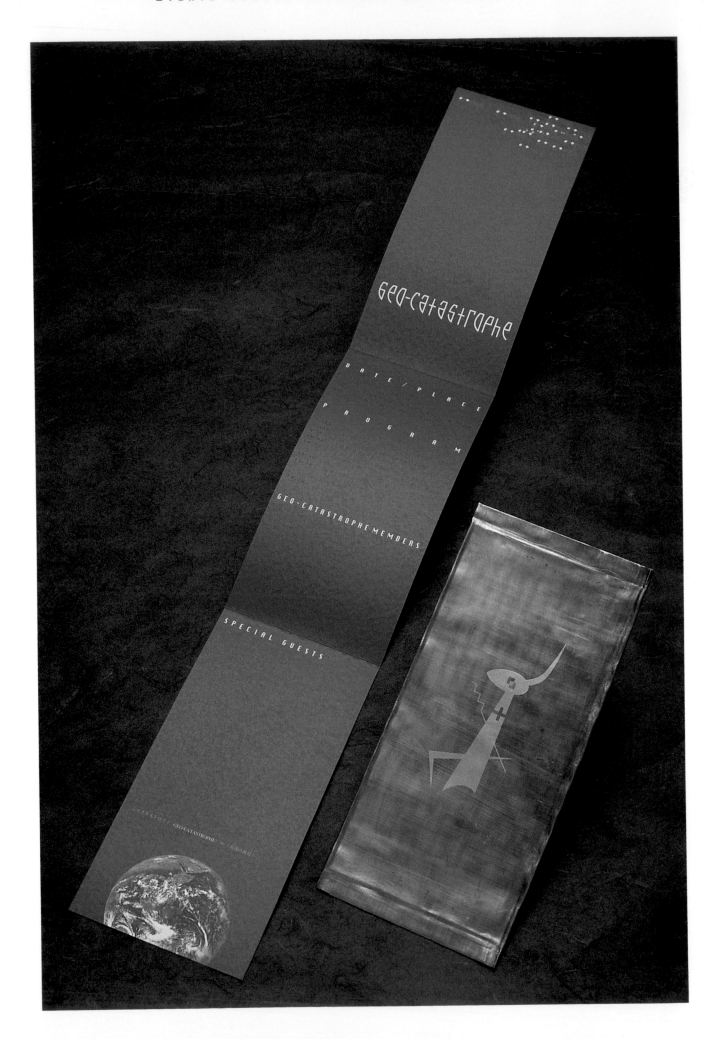

(THIS SPREAD) ART DIRECTOR: MASAYUKI SHIMIZU DESIGNERS: MASAYUKI SHIMIZU, NIO KIMURA PHOTOGRAPHER: KATUZI NISIKAWA
AGENCY: CN CORPORATION CLIENT: OSAKA GAS RESEARCH INSTITUTE FOR CULTURE, ENERGY AND LIFE (CEL) COUNTRY: JAPAN

(ABOVE LEFT) ART DIRECTOR/DESIGNER: SAM KUO STUDIO/CLIENT: KUO DESIGN OFFICE COUNTRY: USA □ (ABOVE RIGHT) ART DIRECTOR/DESIGNER: VALERIE WONG ASSISTANT DESIGNER: CARY CHIAO PHOTOGRAPHER: TOM LANDECKER AGENCY: THE DESIGN OFFICE OF WONG & YEO CLIENT: KATE FOLEY COMPANY COUNTRY: USA □ (ABOVE BOTTOM) ART DIRECTOR/DESIGNER: DOUG TRAPP COPYWRITER: CORINNE MITCHELL AGENCY: McCOOL & COMPANY CLIENT: BARRY McCOOL COUNTRY: USA □ (OPPOSITE) ART DIRECTOR: ROBERT PETRICK DESIGNER: LAURA RESS PHOTOGRAPHER: FRANÇOIS ROBERT AGENCY: PETRICK DESIGN CLIENT: DIFFA (DESIGN INDUSTRY FOUNDATION FIGHTING AIDS) COUNTRY: USA

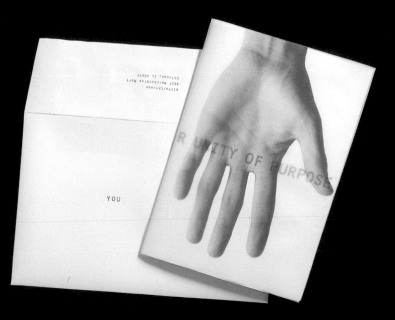

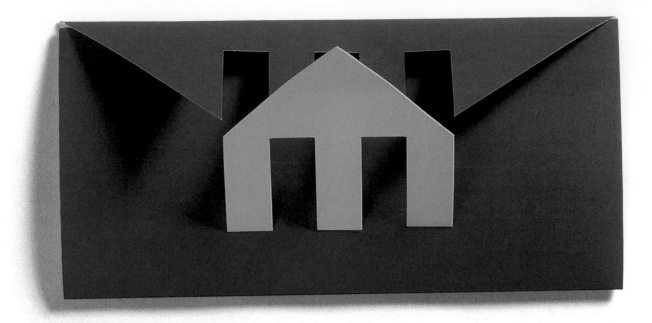

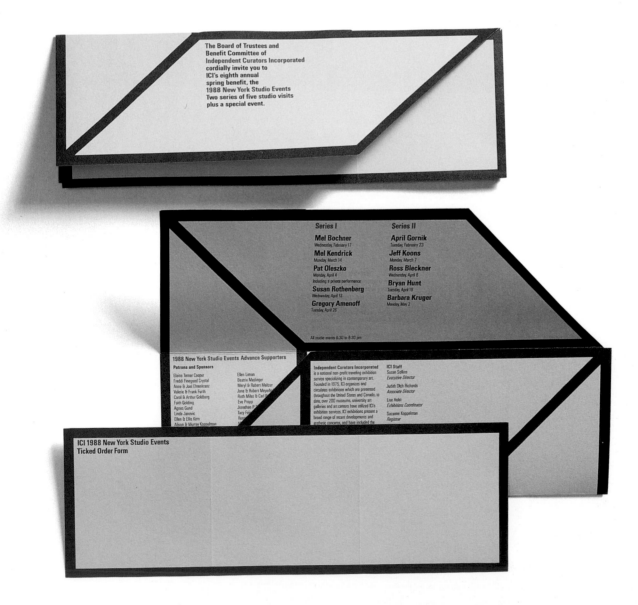

The Board of Trustees and
Benefit Committee of
Independent Curators Incorporated
cordially invite you to
ICI's eighth annual
spring benefit, the
1988 New York Studio Events
Two series of five studio visits
plus a special event.

Series I	Series II
Mel Bochner	**April Gornik**
Wednesday, February 17	Tuesday, February 23
Mel Kendrick	**Jeff Koons**
Monday, March 14	Monday, March 7
Pat Oleszko	**Ross Bleckner**
Monday, April 4	Wednesday, April 6
Including a private performance	
Susan Rothenberg	**Bryan Hunt**
Wednesday, April 13	Tuesday, April 19
Gregory Amenoff	**Barbara Kruger**
Tuesday, April 26	Monday, May 2

All studio events 6:30 to 8:30 pm

1988 New York Studio Events Advance Supporters

Patrons and Sponsors

Elaine Terner Cooper
Freddi Feirgrad Crystal
Anne & Joel Ehrenkranz
Valerie & Frank Furth
Carol & Arthur Goldberg
Faith Golding
Agnes Gund
Linda Janovic
Ellen & Ellis Kern
Alison & Murray Koppelman

Ellen Loman
Beatrix Medinger
Meryl & Robert Meltzer
Jane & Robert Meyerhoff
Ruth Miles & Carl G
Eve Propp
Jonathan P. B
Tracy Feigel
Ros

Independent Curators Incorporated
is a national non-profit traveling exhibition
service specializing in contemporary art.
Founded in 1975, ICI organizes and
circulates exhibitions which are presented
throughout the United States and Canada; to
date, over 200 museums, university art
galleries and art centers have utilized ICI's
exhibition services. ICI exhibitions present a
broad range of recent developments and
aesthetic concerns, and have included the

ICI Staff
Susan Sollins
Executive Director

Judith Olch Richards
Associate Director

Lisa Hahn
Exhibitions Coordinator

Suzanne Koppelman
Registrar

**ICI 1988 New York Studio Events
Ticked Order Form**

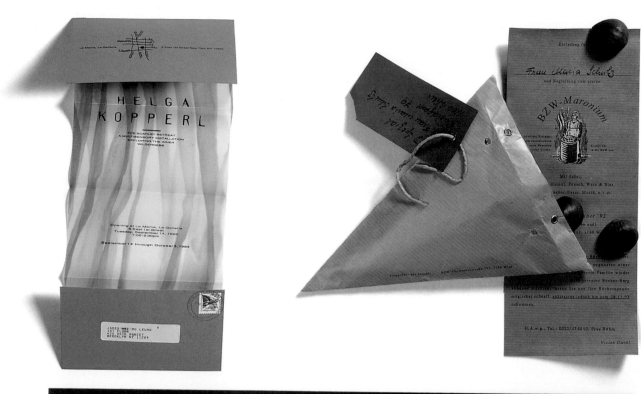

(OPPOSITE PAGE TOP) ART DIRECTOR: HEIKE JANSEN DESIGNERS: HEIKE JANSEN, MICHAEL MARSCHALL CLIENT: DEUTSCHE BANK BAUSPAR AG COUNTRY: GERMANY □ (OPPOSITE PAGE BOTTOM) ART DIRECTORS: MICHAEL MCGINN, TAKAAKI MATSUMOTO DESIGNER: MICHAEL MCGINN AGENCY: M PLUS M INCORPORATED CLIENT: INDEPENDENT CURATORS INC. COUNTRY: USA □ (THIS PAGE TOP LEFT) ART DIRECTOR: JAMES WAI MO LEUNG DESIGNER: JAMES WAI MO LEUNG AGENCY: JAMES LEUNG DESIGN CLIENT: HELGA KOPPERL COUNTRY: USA □ (THIS PAGE TOP RIGHT) ART DIRECTOR: WOLFGANG HASLINGER DESIGNER: WOLFGANG HASLINGER ILLUSTRATOR: WOLFGANG HASLINGER CLIENT: BZW-WERBEAGENTUR COUNTRY: AUSTRIA □ (THIS PAGE BOTTOM) ART DIRECTOR: DESIGNER: SUSANNE AHLERS AGENCY: RG WIESMEIER WERBEAGENTUR GMBH CLIENT: OP COUTURE BRILLEN GMBH COUNTRY: GERMANY

(THIS PAGE TOP LEFT) ART DIRECTOR/DESIGNER: EDUARD CEHOVIN CLIENT: EDUARD CEHOVIN COUNTRY: SLOVENIA □ (THIS PAGE TOP RIGHT) ART DIRECTOR: ANTONIO ROMANO PHOTOGRAPHER: GIUSEPPE MARIA FADDA AGENCY: AR&A ANTONIO ROMANO & ASSOCIATI CLIENT: FINMECCANICA COUNTRY: ITALY □ (ABOVE CENTER) ART DIRECTOR/DESIGNER: DAGMAR SCHROEBLER AGENCY: RG WIESMEIER WERBEAGENTUR GMBH CLIENT: PANAMA JACK COUNTRY: SPAIN □ (ABOVE BOTTOM LEFT) ART DIRECTORS: JÉRÔME OUDIN, SUSANNA SHANNON DESIGNERS: JÉRÔME OUDIN, SUSANNA SHANNON AGENCY: DESIGN DEPT. CLIENT: STAFF P.E.L. ET CALYPSO COUNTRY: FRANCE □ (THIS PAGE BOTTOM RIGHT) ART DIRECTOR/DESIGNER: VERONIKA KYRAL AGENCY: VERONIKA KYRAL CLIENT: FA. LUDWIG KYRAL COUNTRY: AUSTRIA

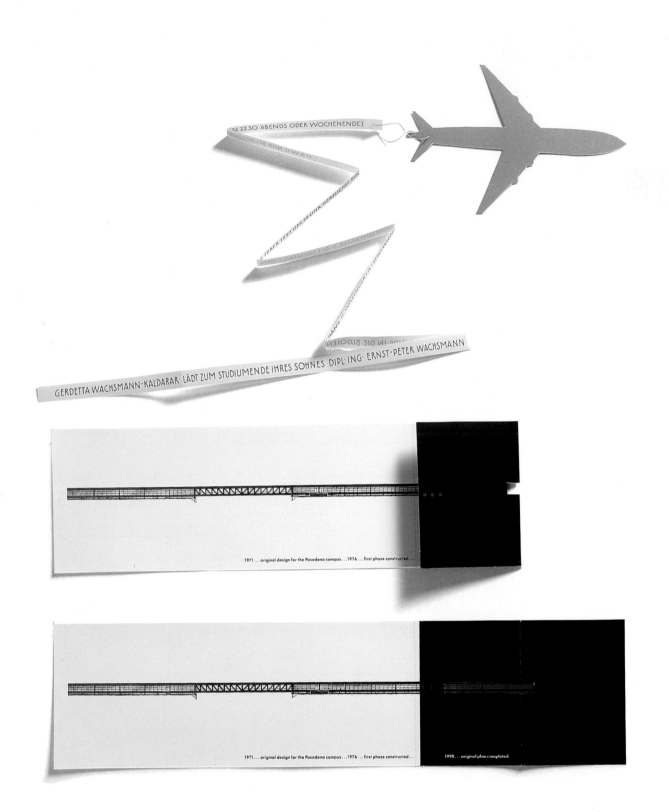

(ABOVE TOP) ART DIRECTOR/DESIGNER/ILLUSTRATOR/AGENCY: VERONIKA KYRAL CLIENT: WACHSMANN COUNTRY: AUSTRIA □ (ABOVE BOTTOM) ART DIRECTOR: REBECA MENDEZ DESIGNER: SZE TSUNG LEONG AGENCY: ART CENTER COLLEGE OF DESIGN OFFICE CLIENT: ART CENTER COLLEGE OF DESIGN COUNTRY: USA □ (OPPOSITE) ART DIRECTOR: KIT HINRICHS DESIGNER: MARK SELFE PHOTOGRAPHER: BARRY ROBINSON ART: KIT HINRICHS AGENCY: PENTAGRAM DESIGN CLIENTS: SAN FRANCISCO MOMA, SAN FRANCISCO ARCHITECTURAL FOUNDATION, MUSEUM ARTS COUNCIL COUNTRY: USA

BEAUX
ARTS
BALL
1993

AN INVITATION

A benefit for the SFMOMA
Department of Architecture and Design

The American Institute of Architects
San Francisco Chapter
The Architectural Foundation of San Francisco
The Modern Art Council of the
San Francisco Museum of Modern Art
cordially invite you to attend the

BEAUX ARTS BALL 1993

...y April 21, 1993
...at San Francisco
...al Reserve Building
...ween Sacramento and Clay

...igning of Museum Girder
... Dinner
...le, judging, and prizes
...table centerpieces closes
...st table design

...by

...Tie

...sponsors, the
...sler Corporation
...cisco

DESIGNERS &
40
ARCHITECTS

Join 40 of San Francisco's
top architects and designers for dinner and
costume ball to celebrate the "Topping Out"
and completion of the structure of the San Francisco
Museum of Art's new building.

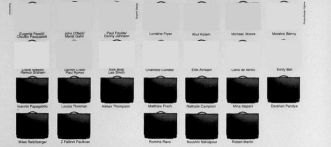

WEST THAMES COLLEGE DIPLOMA SHOW. ADVERTISING & GRAPHIC DESIGN: Villa Carlotta 39 Charlotte St. W1.
Tuesday 21 June Private View 6-9. Open to the public Wednesday 22 June 10-5.30 RSVP 081 568 0244 x 217.

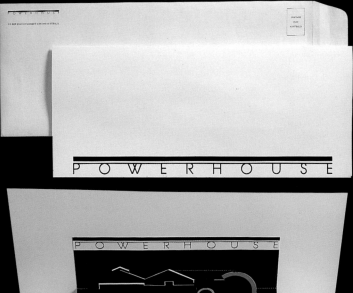

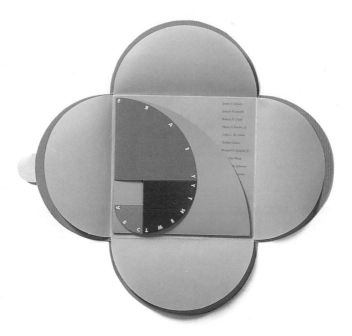

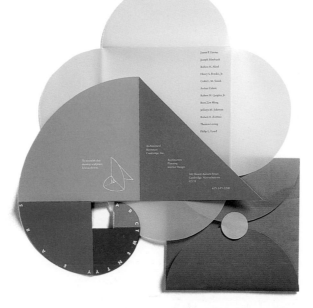

(OPPOSITE TOP) ART DIRECTOR/DESIGNER/COPYWRITER: MICHAEL McPHERSON AGENCY: COREY McPHERSON NASH CLIENT: ARCHI-
TECTURAL RESOURCES CAMBRIDGE COUNTRY: USA □ (OPPOSITE CENTER) ART DIRECTOR/DESIGNER: JOHN SPATCHURST
AGENCY: SPATCHURST DESIGN ASSOC. CLIENT: ART GALLERY OF NEW SOUTH WALES COUNTRY: AUSTRALIA □
(OPPOSITE BOTTOM) ART DIRECTOR/DESIGNER: COLIN JAMES ROWAN ILLUSTRATOR: EMERY VINCENT ASSOC. AGENCY: JANE
SILVER SMITH CLIENT: MINISTRY OF THE ARTS COUNTRY: AUSTRALIA □ (ABOVE) ART DIRECTOR: VINCENT McEVOY
DESIGNER: VINCENT McEVOY PHOTOGRAPHER: ALISTAIR OGILVIE CLIENT: WEST THAMES COLLEGE COUNTRY: GREAT BRITAIN

Vážený spoluobčane! Posíláme Vám na ukázku tzv. *malířský klínek*, nezbytnou součást moderních tendencí v malířství nejen XX. století. Klínky tohoto či téměř shodného tvaru používali mistři palety a štětce, jejichž jména čítáme v těch nejnedostupnějších katalozích, stejně jako ti, jejichž jména v týchž katalozích postrádáme, jimiž se ale hemží katalogy zbytečné a nezajímavé. Klínků shodných s tímto vzorkem užívá rovněž mladá malířka **IRENA WAGNEROVÁ**, o čemž se můžete přesvědčit na její 4. samostatné výstavě, pořádané Aktivem mladých výtvarníků ve spolupráci s SČVU, **v Galerii mladých** (U Řečických) v Praze 1, Vodičkově ulici 10, ve dnech od 25. října do 5. listopadu 1989, nejlépe však při slavnostním zahájení **25. října v 17 hodin.** Hostem Ireny Wagnerové je malířka **Dorota Zlatohlávková**. Výstava je otevřena denně mimo pondělí v 10–13 a v 14–18 hodin. Těšíme se na Vaši návštěvu.

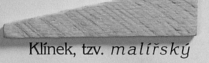

Klínek, tzv. *malířský*

Ukázka praktického *použití klínku* v případě Ireny Wagnerové:

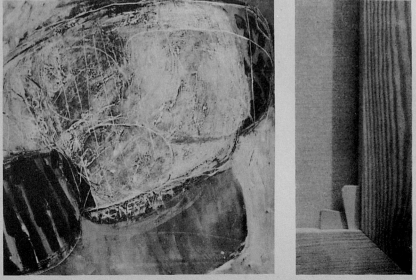

Na obraze z cyklu „Kameny a mušle" (olej, 1988, 29 ½ × 29 ½") není klínek zpředu vidět,... ale detail zadní strany obrazu hovoří jasně!

(OPPOSITE) ART DIRECTOR/DESIGNER: PAVEL BENES PHOTOGRAPHERS: JAN SILPOCH, W.C. CULVER AGENCY: GRAPHIC DESIGN PAVEL
BENES CLIENT: IRENA WAGNEROVA COUNTRY: CZECH REPUBLIC □ (ABOVE) ART DIRECTORS: MICHAEL MCGINN,
TAKAAKI MATSUMOTO DESIGNER: MICHAEL MCGINN AGENCY: M PLUS M INC. CLIENT: INDEPENDENT CURATORS INC. COUNTRY: USA

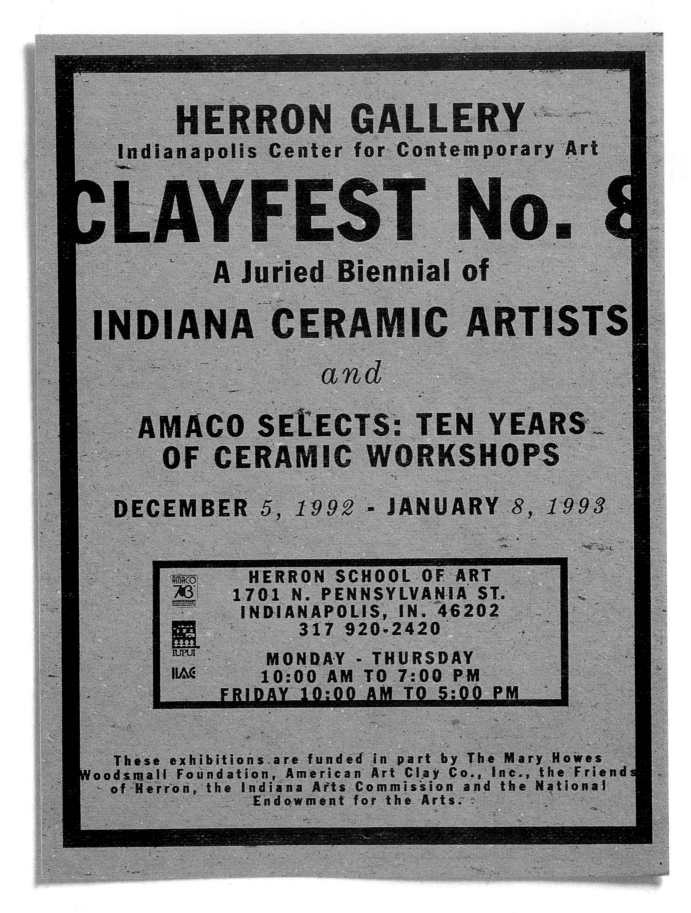

HERRON GALLERY
Indianapolis Center for Contemporary Art
CLAYFEST No. 8
A Juried Biennial of
INDIANA CERAMIC ARTISTS
and
AMACO SELECTS: TEN YEARS OF CERAMIC WORKSHOPS

DECEMBER *5, 1992* - JANUARY *8, 1993*

HERRON SCHOOL OF ART
1701 N. PENNSYLVANIA ST.
INDIANAPOLIS, IN. 46202
317 920-2420

MONDAY - THURSDAY
10:00 AM TO 7:00 PM
FRIDAY 10:00 AM TO 5:00 PM

These exhibitions are funded in part by The Mary Howes
Woodsmall Foundation, American Art Clay Co., Inc., the Friends
of Herron, the Indiana Arts Commission and the National
Endowment for the Arts.

(ABOVE) DESIGNER: JIM ROSS AGENCY: MIRELEZ/ROSS CLIENT: HERRON GALLERY COUNTRY: USA □ (OPPOSITE) ART DIRECTOR/
DESIGNER: AMY MCFARLAND PHOTOGRAPHER: BARBARA LYTER CLIENT: LOS ANGELES COUNTY MUSEUM OF ART COUNTRY: USA

When Art Became Fashion:
KOSODE IN EDO-PERIOD JAPAN

—— I/We accept the invitation for
Wednesday evening, November 11, 1992.

—— I/We regret.

Please print name(s)

A dynamic urban culture flourished in Edo-period Japan (1615–1868), leaving a legacy of plays and novels, woodblock prints, and extraordinary designs on clothing. An escape from mundane concerns was provided by the kabuki theaters and pleasure quarters of the "floating world," where actors and highly refined courtesans set fashion for all levels of society.

The primary garment of both men and women in Edo-period Japan was the kosode, predecessor of the modern kimono. The kosode, the graphic potential of which was exploited by highly skilled artisans, became a "canvas" moving in three-dimensional space. Possessing a complex integration of design and form, the often elaborately decorated kosode expressed the same aesthetic characteristics that infused all the arts produced under the rule of the Tokugawa shogunate. More than two hundred works, including kosode, obi, genre paintings, and woodblock-printed pattern books, shown in two rotations, represent this flowering of the textile arts of Japan.

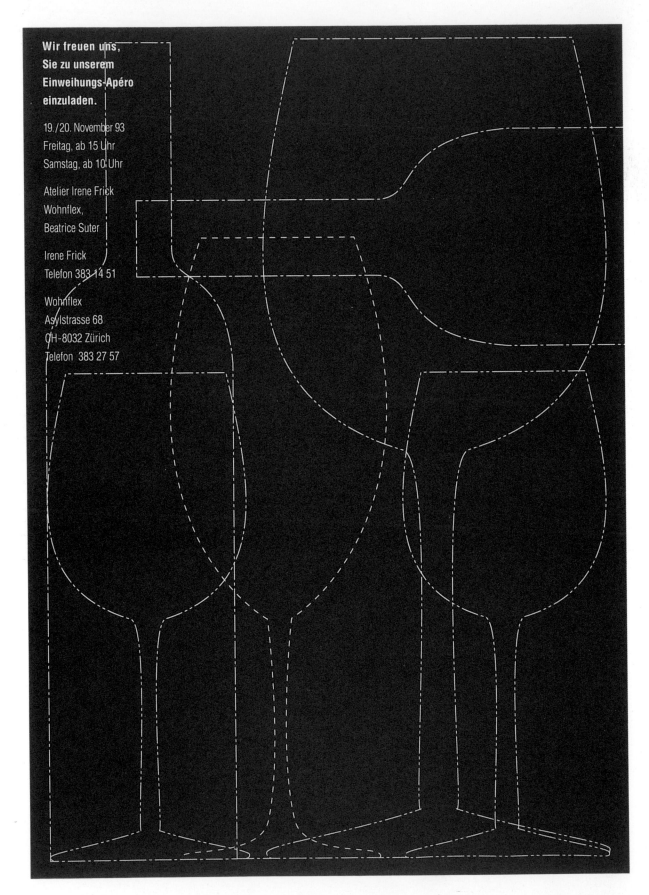

**Wir freuen uns,
Sie zu unserem
Einweihungs-Apéro
einzuladen.**

19./20. November 93
Freitag, ab 15 Uhr
Samstag, ab 10 Uhr

Atelier Irene Frick
Wohnflex,
Beatrice Suter

Irene Frick
Telefon 383 14 51

Wohnflex
Asylstrasse 68
CH-8032 Zürich
Telefon 383 27 57

AIGA/LA invites you to an evening with
Jennifer Morla, President and Creative
Director of Morla Design, a multi-faceted
design firm offering creative services which
encompass print collateral, identity design,
video art direction and design, packaging,
architectural design, and signage. Recent
projects include animation for MTV, national
department store interior design programs
for Levi Strauss, SWATCH Watch designs, and
extensive identity campaigns for experimen-
tal art organizations and museums.
Wednesday, June 16: 6:30pm reception, 7:30pm
speaking engagement. Pacific Design Center,
Center Green Theatre, Floor Two, 8687 Melrose
Avenue, West Hollywood, California 90069.
RSVP by Monday, June 14, by check to:
AIGA/LA, 620 Moulton Avenue #211, Los
Angeles, California 90031, 310.364.1788.

Design is
seductive
propaganda
Morla
AIGA/LA
6.16.93

Sponsors: Color, Inc.,
Gilbert Paper, James
River Premium Printing
Papers **Patrons:** Alan
Lithograph, Inc., An-
derson Lithograph,
Andresen Graphic
Services, Burdge, Inc.,
Color Service, Inc.,
Donahue Printing Com-
pany, Electric
Pencil, G.P.Color,
George Rice & Sons,
Graphic Arts Center,
Klearfold, L.A. Filmco,
Inc., L.A. Fonts Typo-
graphy, Lithographix,
Inc., Santa Monica Mic-
roAge, Stat House/Col-
ortone House, Tech-
tron/LosAngeles,

A. *Jonathan Combs*
   Scratchboard & airbrush
B. *Bill Cannon*
   Photograph
C. *David Harto*
   Airbrush ink & gouache
D. *Kathlyn Shedle*
   Scratchboard & dyes
E. *Chuck Pyle*
   Oil
F. *Steve Coppin*
   Airbrush ink
G. *Vikki Leib*
   Computer
H. *Larry Duke*
   Scratchboard & watercolor
I. *John C. Smith*
   Computer
J. *Bobbi Tull*
   Watercolor
K. *Elizabeth Read*
   Scratchboard & watercolor
L. *Dennis Ochsner*
   Colored pencil
M. *Bruce Morser*
   Pencil

(OPPOSITE) ART DIRECTOR/DESIGNER: KEISUKE UNOSAWA AGENCY/CLIENT: KEISUKE UNOSAWA DESIGN COUNTRY: JAPAN □ (ABOVE) ART DIRECTORS/DESIGNERS: JANET KRUSE, TRACI DABERKO ARTISTS (FROM LEFT TO RIGHT): JONATHAN COMBS, BILL CANNON, DAVID HARTO AGENCY: THE LEONHARDT GROUP CLIENT: PAT HACKETT ARTIST REPRESENTATIVE COUNTRY: USA

(ABOVE) ART DIRECTOR: JARED SCHNEIDMAN DESIGNER: GUILBERT GATES ILLUSTRATORS: JARED SCHNEIDMAN, GUILBERT
GATES, KATHLEEN KATIMS AGENCY: JARED SCHNEIDMAN DESIGN COUNTRY: USA □ (OPPOSITE PAGE TOP) ART
DIRECTORS: STEVEN JINEL, FRÉDÉRIC BOSSER DESIGNER: STEVEN JINEL AGENCY: CAPONE CLIENT: ETUDE
BOISGIRARD COUNTRY: FRANCE □ (OPPOSITE PAGE BOTTOM) ILLUSTRATOR: ERHARD HÖNICKE COUNTRY: SWITZERLAND

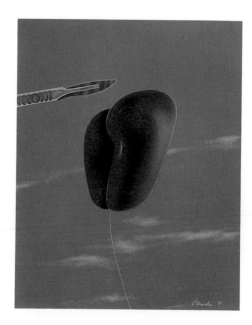

(ABOVE) ART DIRECTOR: FRITZ W. WURSTER DESIGNERS: SABINE RENNER, LESLIE SPEER PHOTOGRAPHERS: JENS WERLEIN, FRITZ W. WURSTER AGENCY/CLIENT: INDUSTRIAL DESIGNERS, FRITZ W. WURSTER COUNTRY: GERMANY □ (OPPOSITE) ART DIRECTOR: STEVE TOLLESON DESIGNERS: STEVE TOLLESON, MARK WINN AGENCY: TOLLESON DESIGN CLIENT: COTTONG + TANIGUCHI COUNTRY: USA

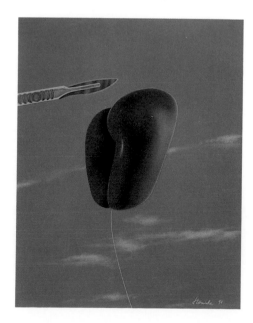

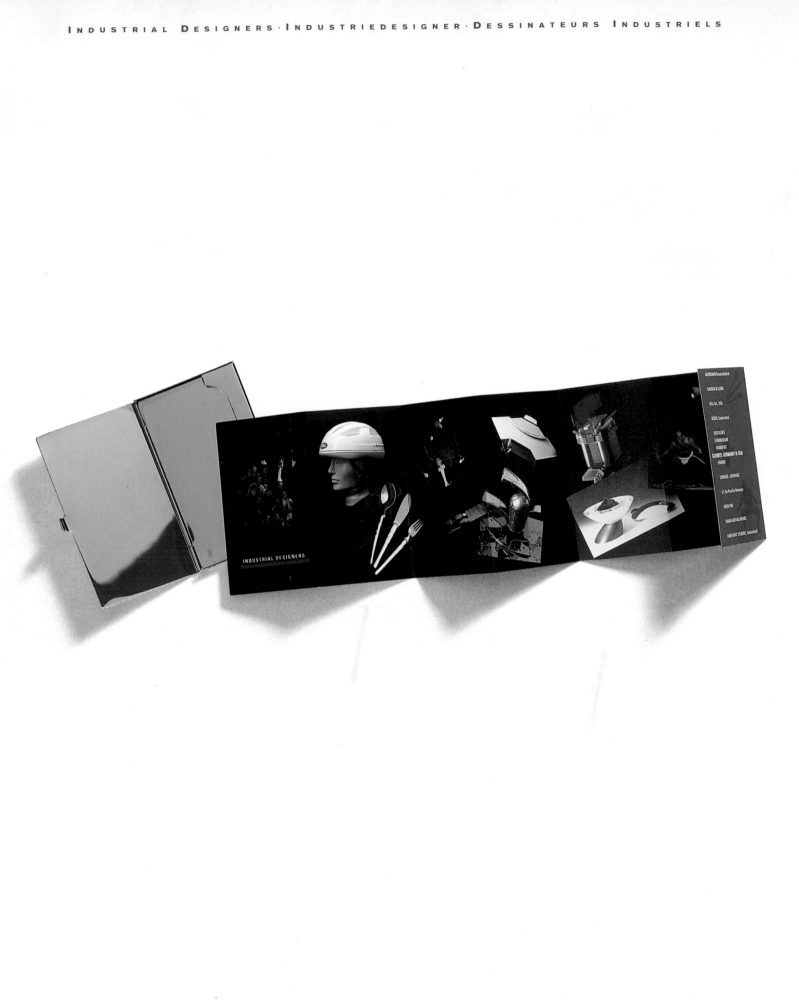

(Above) ART DIRECTOR: FRITZ W. WURSTER DESIGNERS: SABINE RENNER, LESLIE SPEER PHOTOGRAPHERS: JENS WERLEIN, FRITZ W. WURSTER AGENCY/CLIENT: INDUSTRIAL DESIGNERS, FRITZ W. WURSTER COUNTRY: GERMANY □ (OPPOSITE) ART DIRECTOR: STEVE TOLLESON DESIGNERS: STEVE TOLLESON, MARK WINN AGENCY: TOLLESON DESIGN CLIENT: COTTONG + TANIGUCHI COUNTRY: USA

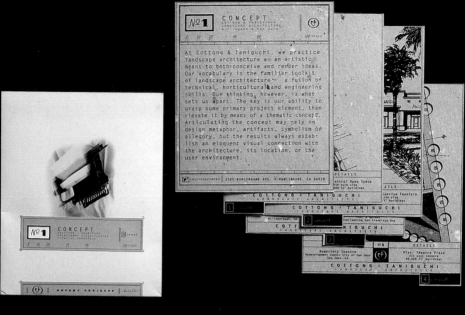

Nº1 CONCEPT

COTTONG & TANIGUCHI
LANDSCAPE ARCHITECTS
Burlingame & San José

At Cottong & Taniguchi, we practice landscape architecture as an artistic means to both conceive and render ideas. Our vocabulary is the familiar toolkit of landscape architecture— a fusion of technical, horticultural and engineering skills. Our thinking, however, is what sets us apart. The key is our ability to grasp some primary project element, then elevate it by means of a thematic concept. Articulating the concept may rely on design metaphor, artifacts, symbolism or allegory, but the results always establish an eloquent visual connection with the architecture, its location, or the user environment.

(415)•342•9063   2165 BURLINGAME AVE. • BURLINGAME, CA 94010

COTTONG • TANIGUCHI
LANDSCAPE ARCHITECTS

Nº1 CONCEPT

RECENT PROJECTS | details

Nº2 BALANCE

RECENT PROJECTS | details

Nº4 STRUCTURE

RECENT PROJECTS | details

Nº3 INTERACTION

RECENT PROJECTS | details

INDUSTRY·INDUSTRIE

(OPPOSITE) ART DIRECTOR: CHARLES HIVELY DESIGNER: CHARLES HIVELY AGENCY: THE HIVELY AGENCY CLIENT: ADMINISTAFF COUNTRY: USA □ (THIS PAGE) ART DIRECTORS: FRANCES NEWELL, JOHN SORRELL DESIGNER: MARK-STEEN ADAMSON AGENCY: NEWELL AND SORRELL CLIENT: UNION RAILWAYS LIMITED COUNTRY: GREAT BRITAIN

(This page) Art Director: VICKIE SCHAFER Designer: VICKIE SCHAFER Photographer: CAROL KAPLAN STUDIO Agency: SIQUIS, LTD. Client: THE SCHWAB COMPANY Country: USA □ (Opposite page) Art Director/Designer: CHRISTO HOLLOWAY Photographer: RICK BURDA Agency: CLOCKWORK APPLE, INC. Client: MTV Country: USA

(OPPOSITE) ART DIRECTOR/COPYWRITER: CLARE ULTIMO DESIGNER: JULIE HUBNER AGENCY/CLIENT: ULTIMO INC. COUNTRY: USA

□ (ABOVE) ART DIRECTORS: ANTONY REDMAN, THAM KHAI MENG DESIGNERS: ANTONY REDMAN, THAM KHAI MENG

AGENCY: BATEY ADS SINGAPORE CLIENTS: BATEY ADS SINGAPORE, SINGAPORE AIRLINES COUNTRY: SINGAPORE

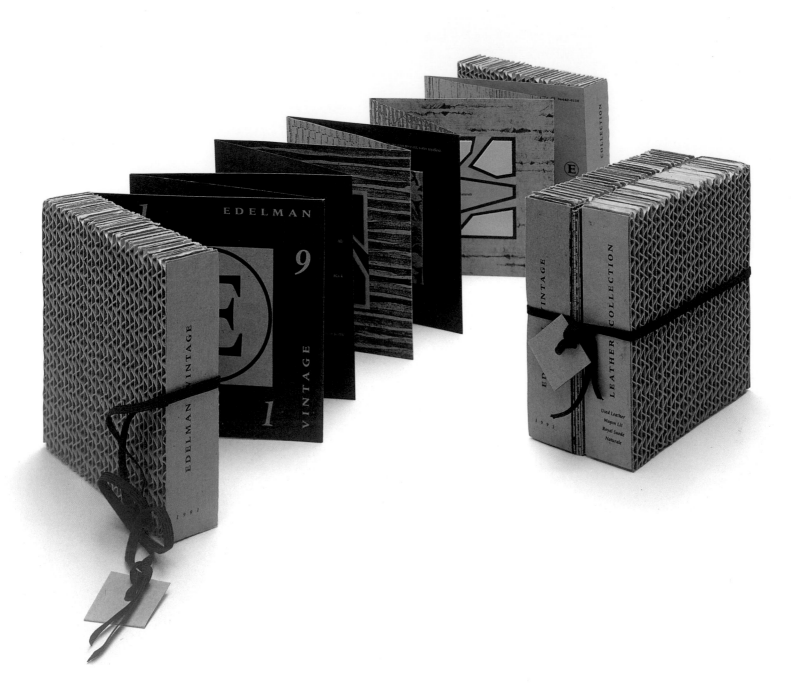

(ABOVE) CREATIVE DIRECTOR/ART DIRECTOR/DESIGNER: MAY LIU COPYWRITER: TEDDY EDELMAN CLIENT: TEDDY & ARTHUR EDELMAN, LTD. COUNTRY: USA □ (OPPOSITE TOP LEFT) ART DIRECTOR: RACHEL MANDEL DESIGNER/ILLUSTRATOR: TRACY SABIN AGENCY: TRACY SABIN GRAPHIC DESIGN CLIENT: HORTON PLAZA COUNTRY: USA □ (TOP RIGHT) ART DIRECTOR: DENNIS ERBER DESIGNER: THOMAS RENK CLIENT: THOMSON C.E. COUNTRY: USA □ (BOTTOM LEFT) ART DIRECTOR: ALAN CHAN DESIGNERS: ALAN CHAN, PETER LO AGENCY: ALAN CHAN DESIGN COMPANY CLIENT: MR. CHAN TEA ROOM LTD. COUNTRY: HONG KONG □ (BOTTOM RIGHT) ART DIRECTOR: CHARLES S. ANDERSON DESIGNERS/ILLUSTRATORS: CHARLES S. ANDERSON, PAUL HOWART AGENCY: CHARLES S. ANDERSON DESIGN CO. CLIENT: TURNER CLASSIC MOVIES COUNTRY: USA

(OPPOSITE) ART DIRECTOR/DESIGNER: ERICH FALKNER COPYWRITER: DR. ANDREAS HOCHSTÖGER AGENCY: GGK WIEN WERBEAGENTUR CLIENT: PORSCHE AUSTRIA GESMBH & CO COUNTRY: AUSTRIA □ (ABOVE TOP) ART DIRECTOR/ DESIGNER: JOHN SWIETER PHOTOGRAPHERS: MAX WEISS AGENCY: SWIETER DESIGN CLIENT: YOUNG PRESIDENTS' ORGANIZATION COUNTRY: USA □ (BOTTOM) ART DIRECTOR: THOMAS G. FOWLER DESIGNERS: THOMAS G. FOWLER, KARL S. MARUYAMA PHOTOGRAPHER: RANDY DUCHAINE AGENCY: TOM FOWLER, INC. CLIENT: H.T. WOODS COUNTRY: USA

(OPPOSITE TOP) ART DIRECTOR: STEFAN OEVERMANN DESIGNER: MARIE-LUISE DORST PHOTOGRAPHER: WALTER SCHELS ILLUSTRATOR:

THOMAS WOBER AGENCY: RG WIESMEIER WERBEAGENTUR CLIENT: CONVATEC BRISTOL-MYERS COUNTRY: GERMANY □

(OPPOSITE BOTTOM AND THIS PAGE) ART DIRECTOR: ALAN CHAN DESIGNERS: ALAN CHAN, CHEN SHUN TSOI ILLUSTRATOR:

ALAN CRACKNEL AGENCY: ALAN CHAN DESIGN CLIENT: MANDARIAN ORIENTAL HK, THE FLOWER SHOP COUNTRY: HONG KONG

(This page top) Art Director: HERIBERT DANKL Designer: HERIBERT DANKL Agency: ADWERBA Client: BMW AUSTRIA BANK Country: AUSTRIA □ (This page bottom left) Art Director: WOLFGANG HASLINGER Designer: WOLFGANG HASLINGER Country: AUSTRIA □ (This page bottom right) Art Director: JAC COVERDALE Designer: JAC COVERDALE Agency: CLARITY COVERDALE FURY ADVERTISING, INC. Client: NORTHWESTERN NATIONAL LIFE Country: USA □ (Opposite page) Art Director: STEVE WEDEEN Designer: STEVE WEDEEN Illustrators: STEVE WEDEEN, CHIP WYLY Agency: VAUGHN WEDEEN CREATIVE Client: US WEST COMMUNICATIONS Country: USA

How many advertising executives does it take to screw in a light bulb?

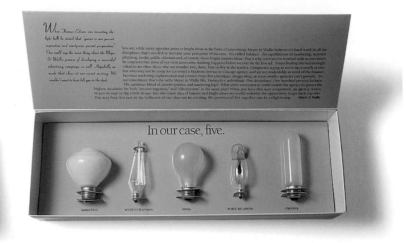

In our case, five.

Unlike many agencies, we're not all talk.

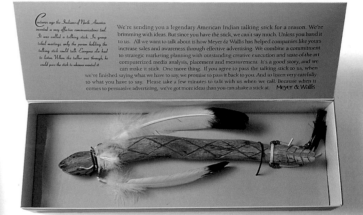

(ABOVE) CREATIVE DIRECTOR: TIM WALLIS ART DIRECTOR: TERRY KRALL COPYWRITER: TIM WALLIS PRODUCER: JULES MILLER AGENCY: MEYER & WALLIS CLIENT: MEYER & WALLIS COUNTRY: USA □ (OPPOSITE) ART DIRECTOR: MARK JOHNSON COPYWRITER: JOHN STINGLEY AGENCY: FALLON MCELLIGOTT CLIENT: FALLON MCELLIGOTT COUNTRY: USA

(OPPOSITE PAGE TOP) ART DIRECTOR: LO BREIER DESIGNER: JÜRG SCHEURER AGENCY/CLIENT: BÜRO X COUNTRY: GERMANY □
(OPPOSITE PAGE BOTTOM) ART DIRECTOR: MICHEL GIRARDIN DESIGNER: MICHEL GIRARDIN PHOTOGRAPHER:
STÉFANIE COUSIN AGENCY/CLIENT: BRUN UND BÜRGIN FOTOGRAFEN SWF COUNTRY: SWITZERLAND □ (THIS PAGE)
ART DIRECTOR/CLIENT: DANIEL HARTZ DESIGNER: FRANZISKA HARTZ ILLUSTRATOR: WERNER HARTZ COUNTRY: GERMANY

(TOP) ART DIRECTOR: ALBERTO BACCARI DESIGNER: TITTI SOFFIANTINO PHOTOGRAPHER: MARIO MONGE AGENCY: ARMANDO
TESTA S.P.A. CLIENT: ARMANDO TESTA S.P.A. COUNTRY: ITALY □ (BOTTOM) ART DIRECTOR/DESIGNER/ILLUSTRATOR:
BBV PROF. MICHAEL BAVIERA AGENCY: BBV PROF. MICHAEL BAVIERA CLIENT: J. HORBER COUNTRY: SWITZERLAND

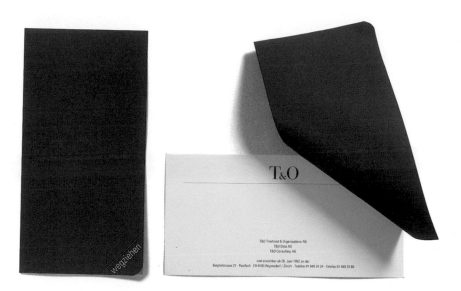

(THIS PAGE TOP) ART DIRECTOR/DESIGNER/ILLUSTRATOR/AGENCY: BBV PROF. MICHAEL BAVIERA CLIENT: T & O TREUHAND COUNTRY: SWITZERLAND □ (THIS PAGE CENTER) ART DIRECTOR: JIMMY YANG DESIGNER: JIMMY YANG PHOTOGRAPHER: NAD NAIM AGENCY/CLIENT: IDENTICA COUNTRY: GREAT BRITAIN □ (THIS PAGE BOTTOM) ART DIRECTOR: ROLAND SCHNEIDER ILLUSTRATOR: MICHAELA BAUER AGENCY: BAUERS BÜRO CLIENT: BAUERS BÜRO COUNTRY: GERMANY

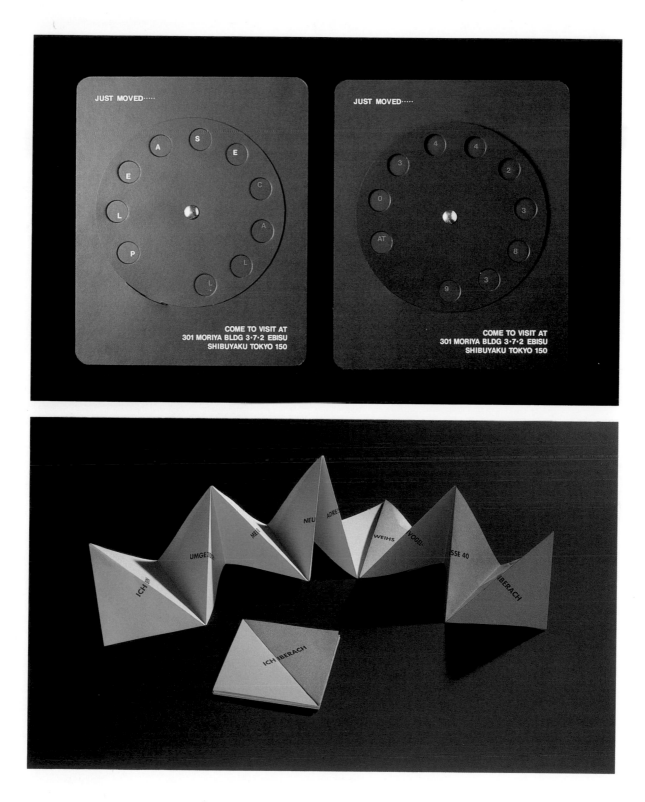

(OPPOSITE PAGE) ART DIRECTORS/DESIGNERS: SUSANNA SHANNON, JÉRÔME SAINT-LOUBERT BIÉ PHOTOGRAPHER: JÉRÔME SAINT-LOUBERT BIÉ AGENCY: DESIGN DEPT. CLIENT: IRREGULAMADAIRE COUNTRY: FRANCE □ (THIS PAGE TOP) ART DIRECTOR: KEISUKE UNOSAWA DESIGNER: KEISUKE UNOSAWA AGENCY/CLIENT: KEISUKE UNOSAWA DESIGN COUNTRY: JAPAN □ (THIS PAGE BOTTOM) DESIGNER: SASCHA WEIHS CLIENT: SASCHA WEIHS COUNTRY: GERMANY

Traslochiamo

da Foro Bonaparte, 63
a via Rugabella, 1

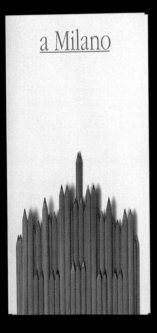

a Milano

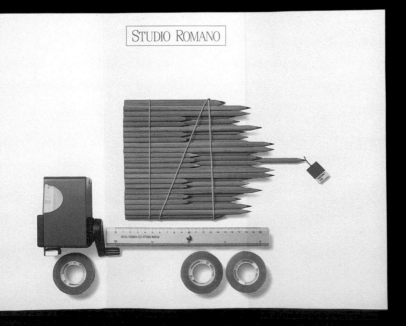

STUDIO ROMANO

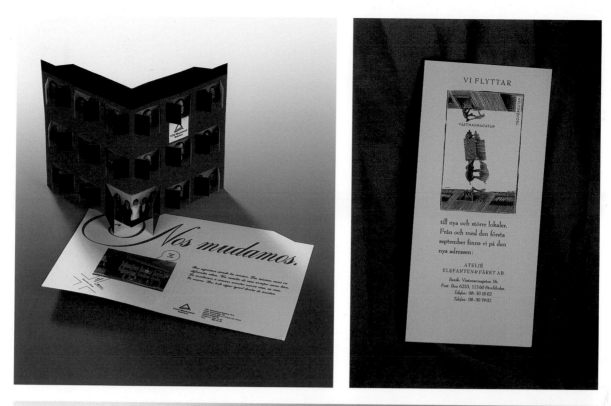

(OPPOSITE PAGE) ART DIRECTOR: ANTONIO ROMANO PHOTOGRAPHER: GIUSEPPE MARIA FADDA AGENCY/CLIENT: AR&A ANTONIO ROMANO & ASSOCIATI COUNTRY: ITALY □ (THIS PAGE TOP LEFT) ART DIRECTOR: KLAUS KRAEGE DESIGNER: KLAUS KRAEGE PHOTOGRAPHER: KLAUS KRAEGE CLIENT: TÜV RHEINLAND IBÉRICA S.A. COUNTRY: SPAIN □ (THIS PAGE TOP RIGHT) ART DIRECTOR: KENNETH KARLSSON DESIGNER: KENNETH KARLSSON ILLUSTRATOR: KENNETH KARLSSON AGENCY/CLIENT: ATELJÉ ELEFANTEN & FARET AB COUNTRY: SWEDEN □ (THIS PAGE BOTTOM) ART DIRECTOR: DOO H. KIM DESIGNERS: DONGIL LEE, JIWON SHIN AGENCY: DOOKIM DESIGN CLIENT: DOOKIM DESIGN COUNTRY: SOUTH KOREA

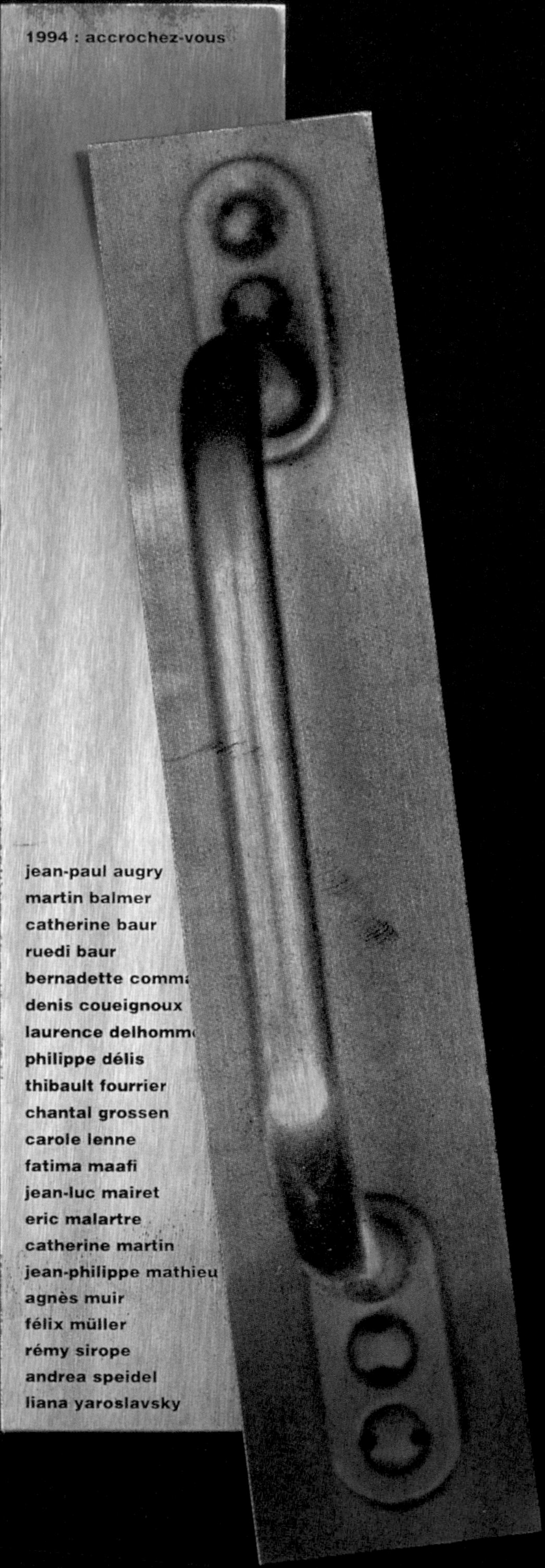

jean-paul augry
martin balmer
catherine baur
ruedi baur
bernadette comma
denis coueignoux
laurence delhomm
philippe délis
thibault fourrier
chantal grossen
carole lenne
fatima maafi
jean-luc mairet
eric malartre
catherine martin
jean-philippe mathieu
agnès muir
félix müller
rémy sirope
andrea speidel
liana yaroslavsky

DEC 31

CELEBRATE
THE BEGINNING
OF THE LAST...

DECADENCE

WILL GET
US THROUGH
THE TIMES
AHEAD.

8 O'CLOCK
AT THE GOODS
RSVP
526-2990

(OPPOSITE PAGE) DESIGNER: RUEDI BAUR AGENCY: INTÉGRAL RUEDI BAUR ET ASSOCIÉS COUNTRY: FRANCE □ (THIS PAGE) ART DIRECTOR: PETER GOOD COPYWRITER: PETER GOOD DESIGNERS: PETER GOOD, JANET GOOD, SUSAN FASICK-JONES AGENCY: PETER GOOD GRAPHIC DESIGN CLIENTS: PETER GOOD, JANET GOOD COUNTRY: USA

(THIS PAGE) ART DIRECTOR: THOMAS G. FOWLER DESIGNER: THOMAS G. FOWLER AGENCY/CLIENT: TOM FOWLER, INC.
COUNTRY: USA □ (OPPOSITE TOP) ART DIRECTOR: BRUNO K. WIESE DESIGNER: BRUNO K. WIESE STUDIO: BK WIESE
VISUAL DESIGN CLIENTS: BRUNO WIESE, RUTH WIESE COUNTRY: GERMANY □ (OPPOSITE BOTTOM) ART DIRECTOR:
ERKEN KAGAROV DESIGNER: ERKEN KAGAROV ILLUSTRATOR: ERKEN KAGAROV AGENCY/CLIENT: IMA-PRESS COUNTRY: RUSSIA

Grüße
zum Jahreswechsel

Turn of the year's
greetings

'93 —

Bruno & Ruth
Wiese

Neues Jahr –
neuer Maßstab

New Year –
new Proportions

— '94

(Above) Art Director: KEITH STEIMEL Designer: CORNERSTONE STAFF Agency/Client: CORNERSTONE DESIGN ASSOCIATES Country: USA □ (Opposite) Art Director: BYRON JACOBS Designers: BYRON JACOBS, TRACY HOI Illustrator: PPA DESIGN LIMITED Agency: PPA DESIGN LIMITED Client: GOLDEN HARVEST FILMS Country: HONG KONG

Victor Dog

The symbol for quality sounds today, and ever since he first appeared in 1927 as the symbol for RCA Victor.

1927년 최초 상표로 출현하여 지금까지 음의 역사를 지키온 견공

MUSEUM DOG

A true masterpiece displaying extraordinary artistic skill, depicting in relief the wild dog of Korea's Chosun Period. (1392-1910)

우리나라 조선시대의 명견으로 응양요원이나 구도, 묘사력에서 매우 뛰어난 솜씨를 보여준 명견

FLANDERS DOG

Loving name given to Patrasche, the loyal friend to a poor youth who dreams of becoming an artist.

화가를 꿈꾸는 가난한 소년과 충실스러운 개 파트라세의 사랑이야기

WINDSOR DOG

The eternally faithful canine companion of the Duke of Windsor, who gave up the throne in the name of love.

사랑을 위해 왕관을 버린 윈저공의 정렬한 충견

MOVIE DOG

A Hollywood super dog-Lassie, a well-known movie star loved by millions.

영화로 주먹으로 사랑을 받았던 영화수 견공 - 헐리우드의 명견 래시

(ALL IMAGES THIS SPREAD) ART DIRECTOR: DOO H. KIM DESIGNERS: DONGIL LEE, JIWON SHIN,
SEUNG HEE LEE AGENCY: DOOKIM DESIGN CLIENT: DOOKIM DESIGN COUNTRY: SOUTH KOREA

(OPPOSITE) ART DIRECTOR/DESIGNER/PHOTOGRAPHER: JEAN-BENOÎT LÉVY AGENCY/CLIENT: AND (TRAFIC GRAFIC) COUNTRY: SWITZERLAND

□ (ABOVE) DESIGNERS: KARIN MEYER, UTE WIEMER COPYWRITER: ROLF TAMMEN AGENCY/CLIENT: TAMMEN GMBH COUNTRY: GERMANY

Entspannende Tage
und
sprühende Ideen
für 1993
wünscht Ihnen
Ihr

HCH · MUERMANN

Team

(THIS PAGE) ART DIRECTOR: ROLAND SCHNEIDER DESIGNER: MICHAELA BAUER AGENCY: BAUERS BÜRO CLIENT:
HCH. MUERMANN GMBH & CO. KG COUNTRY: GERMANY □ (OPPOSITE PAGE) ART DIRECTOR: DOO H. KIM
DESIGNERS: DONGIL LEE. JIWON SHIN AGENCY: DOOKIM DESIGN CLIENT: DOOKIM DESIGN COUNTRY: SOUTH KOREA

Corporate Symbol

Grid System

MONKEY '92 CORPORATE DESIGN MANUAL

Signature & Color Scheme

Incorrected Symbol

MONKEY'92

Monkey Red

Monkey Gray

MONKEY'92

MONKEY'92

MONKEY'92

Tür und Tor

Asterix und Obelix

hoch und heilig

Licht und Schatten

Weihnacht und Neujahr

Alles Gute!

Dirk

Heine: Kampweg 9

3008 Garbsen

Dirk

Heine: Photographie,

Visuelle Kommunikation

(OPPOSITE) ART DIRECTOR/DESIGNER/CLIENT: DIRK HEINE COUNTRY: GERMANY □ (ABOVE) ART DIRECTOR/DESIGNER: MONICA
HEYMANN PHOTOGRAPHER: BRUNO AGENCY: RAIN MAKER ADVERTISING CLIENT: BRUNO PHOTOGRAPHY INC. COUNTRY: USA

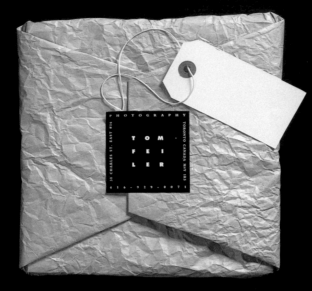

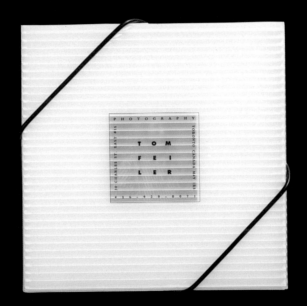

(OPPOSITE PAGE) ART DIRECTOR: MERCEDES ROTHWELL DESIGNER: MERCEDES ROTHWELL PHOTOGRAPHER: TOM FEILER AGENCY: HAMBLY & WOOLLEY INC. CLIENT: TOM FEILER PHOTOGRAPHY COUNTRY: CANADA □ (THIS PAGE) ART DIRECTOR/DESIGNER/COPYWRITER: NEAL ASHBY PHOTOGRAPHER/CLIENT: BARRY MYERS AGENCY: ASHBY DESIGN COUNTRY: USA

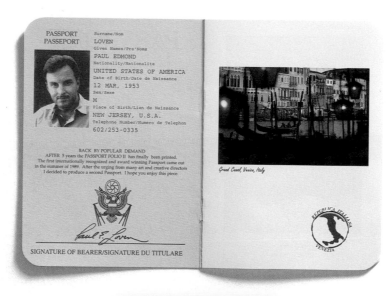

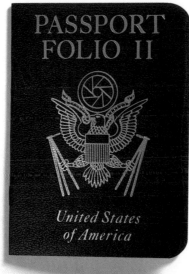

(Opposite) Photographer/Client: Werner Gritzbach Country: Germany □ (Above) Art Director: Randy Palmer
Designers: Ron Leland, Paul Loven Photographer: Paul Loven Client: Paul Loven Photography, Inc. Country: USA

PHOTOGRAPHERS · PHOTOGRAPHEN · PHOTOGRAPHES

(ABOVE) DESIGNER: ANDREW HOYNE PHOTOGRAPHER: ROB BLACKBURN AGENCY: ANDREW HOYNE
DESIGN CLIENT: SUN STUDIO COUNTRY: AUSTRALIA □ (OPPOSITE) ART DIRECTOR/PHOTOG-
RAPHER/CLIENT: COLIN GRAY DESIGNERS: COLIN GRAY, NICKY REGAN COUNTRY: GREAT BRITAIN

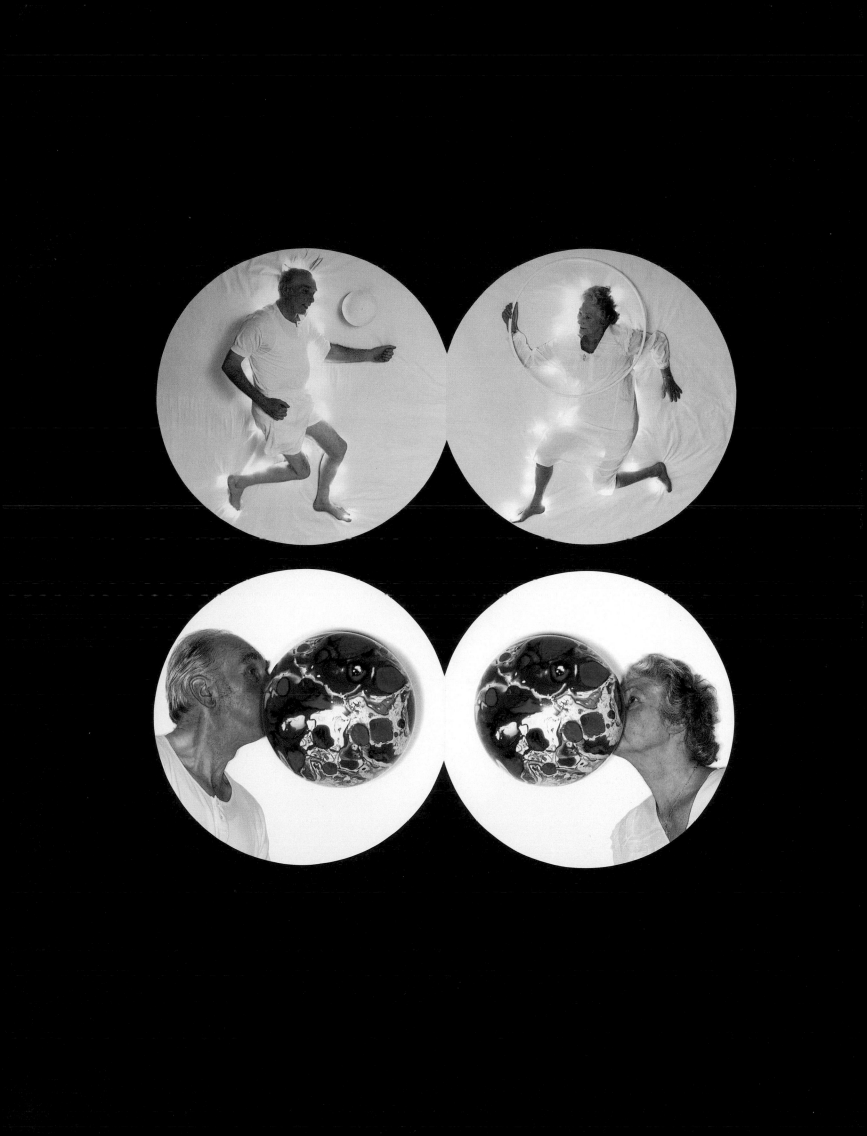

BURKE&FOSTER PRINTING&COPYING

Menu

of Services

OPEN
24 hours

(OPPOSITE) ART DIRECTORS: BOB HAMBLY, BARBARA WOOLLEY, MERCEDES ROTHWELL DESIGNER: MERCEDES ROTHWELL
ILLUSTRATOR: SETH AGENCY: HAMBLY & WOOLLEY CLIENT: BURKE & FOSTER PRINTING & COPYING COUNTRY: CANADA
□ (ABOVE) ART DIRECTOR/DESIGNER/ILLUSTRATOR: WOLFGANG HASLINGER CLIENT: REPROTECHNIK BIBERLE COUNTRY: AUSTRIA

SCOTT GOTHIC
(PRIVATE INVESTIGATOR)

CONFIDENTIAL

(1) FILE NO. 30785
(2) Gripping Typos
(3) CLIENT Andresen Supercomix
(4) VILLAIN Günter Gerhard Lange
DESCRIPTION
AGE — D.O.B. Unknown
HEIGHT 4'11" WEIGHT 185
HAIR COLOR Blk EYE COLOR Gray
IDENTIFYING MARKS Evil look in eyes
(5) FEE $25 a day plus exp.
(6) COMMENTS no problem!

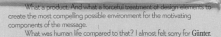

What a product. And what a forceful treatment of design elements to create the most compelling possible environment for the motivating components of the message.
What was human life compared to that? I almost felt sorry for Günter.

Almost. But I had no time for sentiment, anyway. I had a fight on my hands.

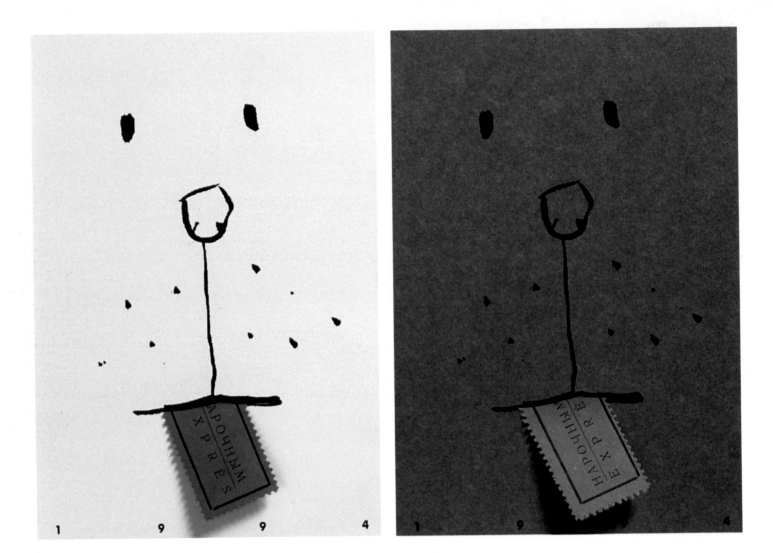

(ABOVE) ART DIRECTOR/DESIGNER/ILLUSTRATOR: ANDREY LOGVIN CLIENT: LINIA GRAFIC COUNTRY: RUSSIA □ (OPPOSITE) ART DIRECTOR:

MAX LEY DESIGNERS: MAX LEY, GERD LANGKAFEL AGENCY: UNIVERS CLIENT: AGFA-COMPUGRAPHIC COUNTRY: GERMANY

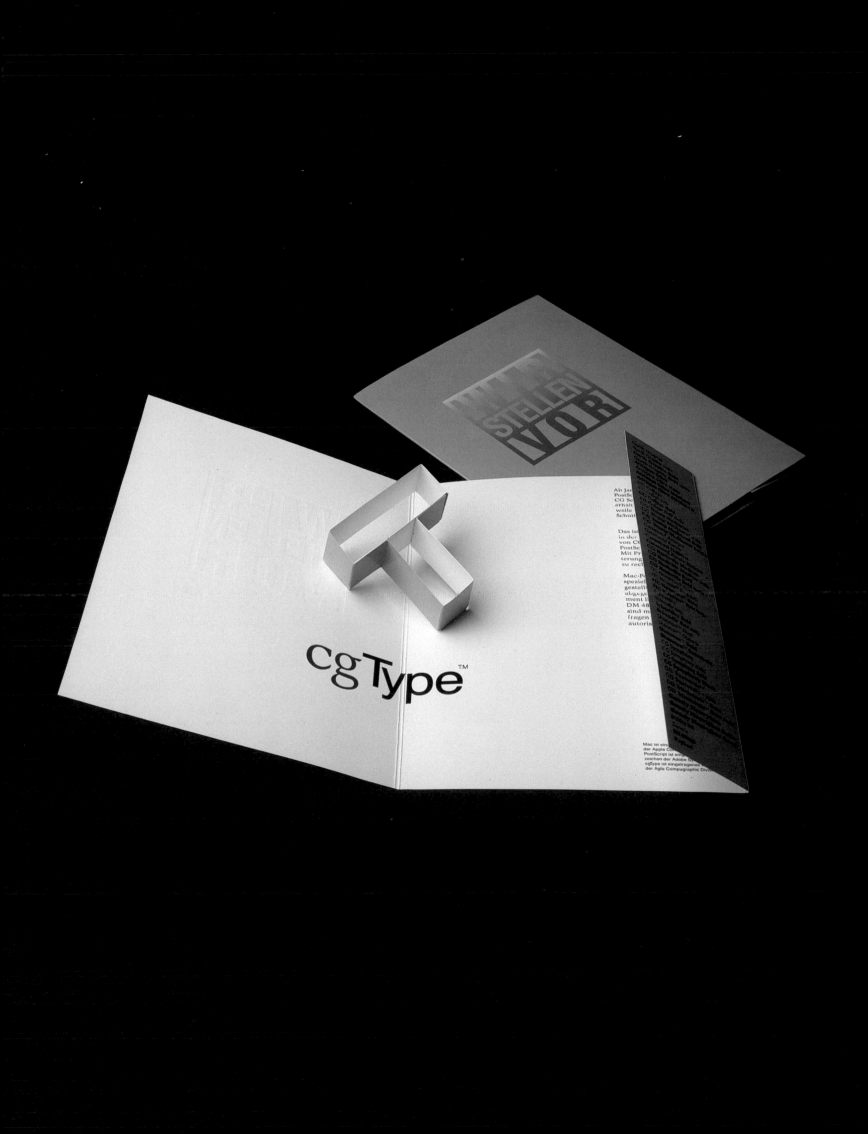

WIR
HEIRATEN

Franziska Rebekka Schmid
&
Daniel Moritz Hartz

AM
4. DEZEMBER 1992

(This page) Designer: FRANZISKA HARTZ Photographer: DANIEL HARTZ Country: GERMANY □ (Opposite page)
Art Worker: PAUL LEBER Illustrator: PAUL LEBER Photographer: HENRIETTE NIELSON Country: SWITZERLAND

TO ENTER DATA

Zajímá-li Vás, o co kráčí, zapište si do svých adresářů následující TEL adresy:

VERONIKA MORAVCOVÁ Famfulíkova 1133, 18200 Praha 8

PAVEL LOUB Kaňkovského 1239, 18200 Praha 8 a stiskněte SET.

TO SPECIFY TIME AND DATE

Co mají ti dva společného . . .?

HOME FUNC FUNC 1

11 TIME/DATE 00 TIME/DATE

9 TIME/DATE 10 TIME/DATE

1993 TIME/DATE SET aneb **9.10.1993 v 11** hodin.

TO USE THE FUNCTION KEY

Tiskněte FUNC tolikrát, kolikrát podle objevivších se neznámých slov uznáte za vhodné. Nedoporučuje se z rozmaru mačkat ALL DELETE, to jde všechno do háje.

TO SEARCH DATA

To není jen tak, zapsat si datum pro nic za nic. Pročež stiskněte TEL Veronika Moravcová a Pavel Loub SEARCH FUNC FUNC 4 DATA COMM 4 1ONE ITEM 1 SEARCH FOR? a vite totéž, co já, čili nic. Ale komu to jen trochu pálí , pochopí, že mají sňatbu, berou se aneb **stanou se svými** ESC.

TO ENTER THE SECRET AREA

🔒 heslo 🔒 , ale je to marné, všichni se to dovědí.

INVITATION FROM

DESIGN © PAVEL BENEŠ, E.D.A., 1993 SET

(THIS PAGE) ART DIRECTOR/DESIGNER: PAVEL BENES AGENCY: GRAPHIC DESIGN PAVEL BENES COUNTRY: CZECH REPUBLIC □ (OPPOSITE PAGE) DESIGNER/ILLUSTRATOR: SASCHA WEIHS COUNTRY: GERMANY

Danièle Baur et
Denis Dall Alba-Arnau
ont le plaisir de
vous faire part de
leur mariage
le 28 septembre 1991.

16h 30 Mairie de Cluses
17h 30 Vin d'honneur
au Forum des Lacs
à Thyez
20h 00 Buffet à la salle
des fêtes
de Châtillon
(rsvp tél: 50 38 39 98)

Danièle Baur et
Denis Dall Alba-Arnau
16 rue de l'Helvétie
74100 Ambilly
tel 50 38 39 98
U+F Baur
Chambéry 79 33 19 15
M. Dall Alba et J. Arnau
Châtillon 50 34 26 53

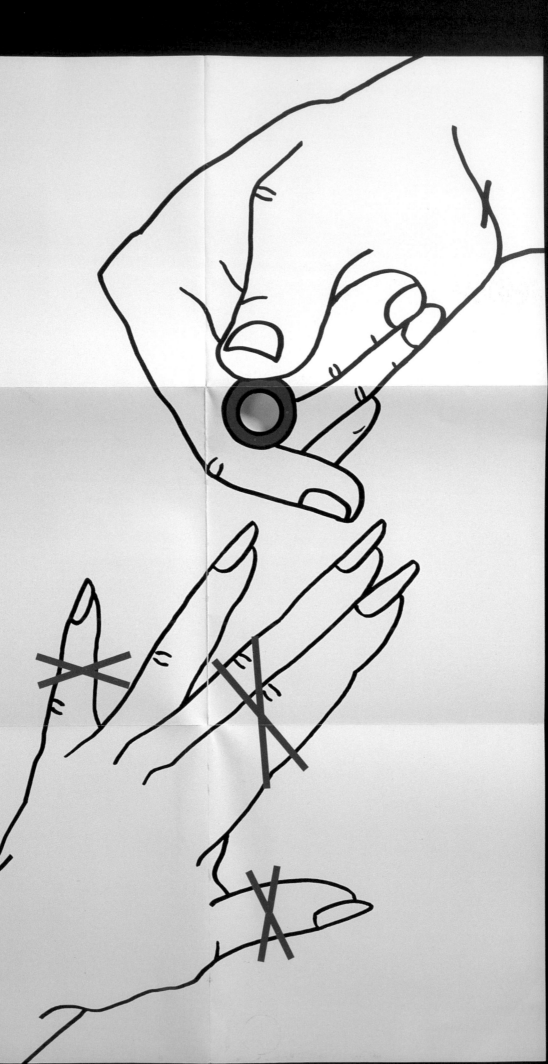

(OPPOSITE) DESIGNER: RUEDI BAUR AGENCY: INTÉGRAL RUEDI BAUR ET ASSOCIÉS COUNTRY: FRANCE □ (ABOVE) ART DIRECTOR/
DESIGNER/ILLUSTRATOR: JOEL TEMPLIN PHOTOGRAPHER: PAUL SINKLER AGENCY: CHARLES S. ANDERSON DESIGN COUNTRY: USA

(THIS PAGE) ART DIRECTOR: MASAYUKI SHIMIZU DESIGNERS: MASAYUKI SHIMIZU, NIO KIMURA AGENCY: HETER-O-DOXY PROTPRAST COUNTRY: JAPAN □ (OPPOSITE PAGE) ART DIRECTORS: WILLIE BARONET, STEVE GIBBS DESIGNERS: WILLIE BARONET, KELLYE KIMBALL, BILL VANCE AGENCY: GIBBS BARONET COUNTRY: USA

...OPQR̶STUVWXYZ

Ron Kostelny and Sheila Baldwin
were married in Dallas
Saturday March 14, 1992 at Holy
Cross Lutheran Church.
The Kostelnys are residing at
3745 Vinecrest, Dallas,
Texas 75229, enjoying a relationship
that is letter perfect.
No gifts, please.

BRUCE HOLDEMAN
AND
MELODY BIGGS
WILL BE MARRIED
ON
SATURDAY,
NOVEMBER 20TH
AT 1:30 PM
AT
FIRST MENNONITE
CHURCH
430 WEST NINTH
AVENUE

COME CELEBRATE
WITH US!

RECEPTION
TO FOLLOW AT
TOURNAMENTS
6075 PARKWAY
DRIVE

(OPPOSITE TOP AND CENTER) ART DIRECTOR/DESIGNER: BRUCE HOLDEMAN AGENCY: 601 DESIGN, INC. COUNTRY: USA □ (OPPOSITE BOTTOM) DESIGNER: LUCA VARASCHINI PHOTOGRAPHER: ANTONIO FANCELLO CLIENT: ANTONIO FANCELLO CALLIGRAPHY: ANNA RONCHI COUNTRY: ITALY □ (THIS PAGE) ART DIRECTOR/DESIGNER: WOLFGANG HASLINGER COUNTRY: AUSTRIA

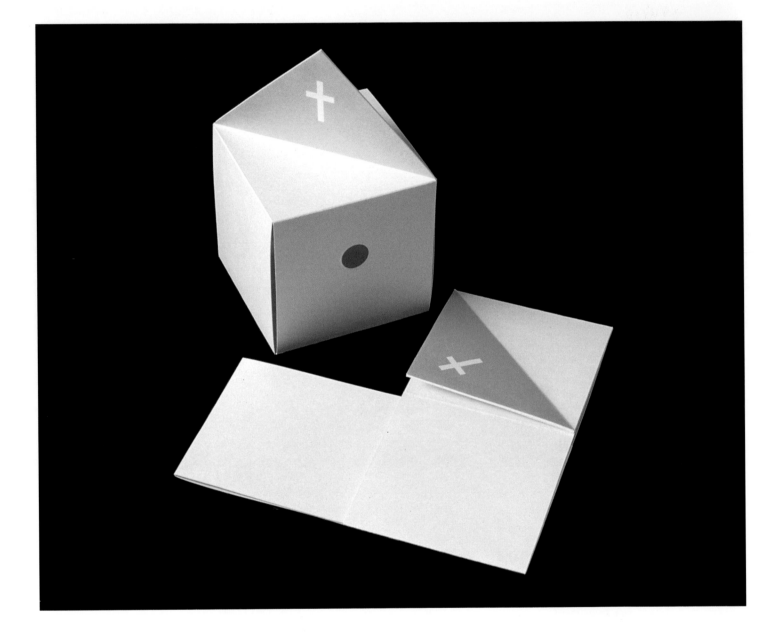

(ABOVE) ART DIRECTOR/DESIGNER: KEISUKE UNOSAWA ILLUSTRATOR: KEISUKE UNOSAWA AGENCY: KESIUKE UNOSAWA DESIGN
COUNTRY: JAPAN □ (OPPOSITE) ART DIRECTOR: ROSE DENDY YOUNG DESIGNER: CAROL DUFFETT COUNTRY: SOUTH AFRICA

קול ששון וקול שמחה ✡ קול חתן וקול כלה

Aaron and Adèle Searll
take great pleasure in inviting you to share
in the celebration of the marriage of their daughter
Catherine Jane
to
Stephen John
son of Jack Abraham & the late Jennifer Abraham
on Sunday 10 April 1994 at
the Gardens Synagogue, Hatfield Street, Cape Town
at 6.30 pm
to be followed by a Dinner Dance
at Monterey, 12-14 Klaassens Road, Bishopscourt.

RSVP: Linda Lee 761-8000 before 18 March 1994
Dress: Black Tie

(ABOVE) DESIGNER: NINA ULMAJA AGENCY: NINA ULMAJA GRAFISK FORM COUNTRY: SWEDEN □ (OPPOSITE) ART DIRECTOR: PAT GORMAN

DESIGNERS: PAT GORMAN, TUNA FLORES ILLUSTRATOR/COPYWRITER: LINDA BARRY AGENCY: PAT GORMAN DESIGN COUNTRY: USA

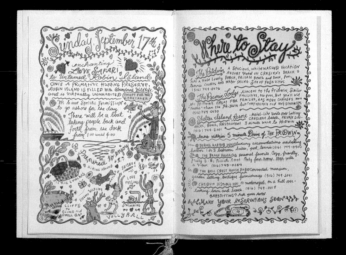

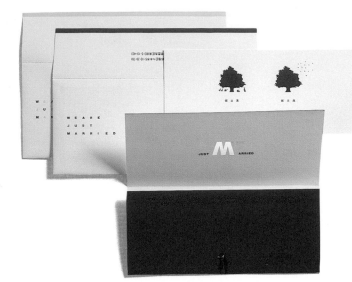

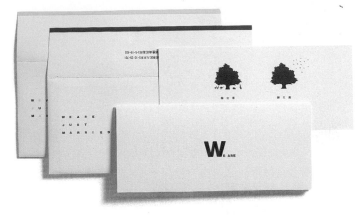

(ABOVE) ART DIRECTOR/DESIGNER: KEISUKE UNOSAWA AGENCY: KEISUKE UNOSAWA DESIGN COUNTRY: JAPAN □ (BOTTOM) DESIGNER/
ILLUSTRATOR: SASCHA WEIHS COUNTRY: GERMANY □ (OPPOSITE TOP) ART DIRECTOR/DESIGNER/COPYWRITER/AGENCY: ROY
CARRUTHERS COUNTRY: USA □ (BOTTOM) ART DIRECTORS/DESIGNERS: GREG MORGAN, CANDACE BUCHANAN COUNTRY: USA

192

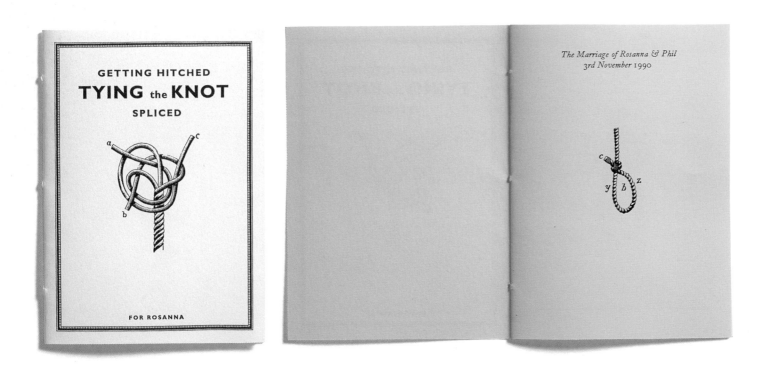

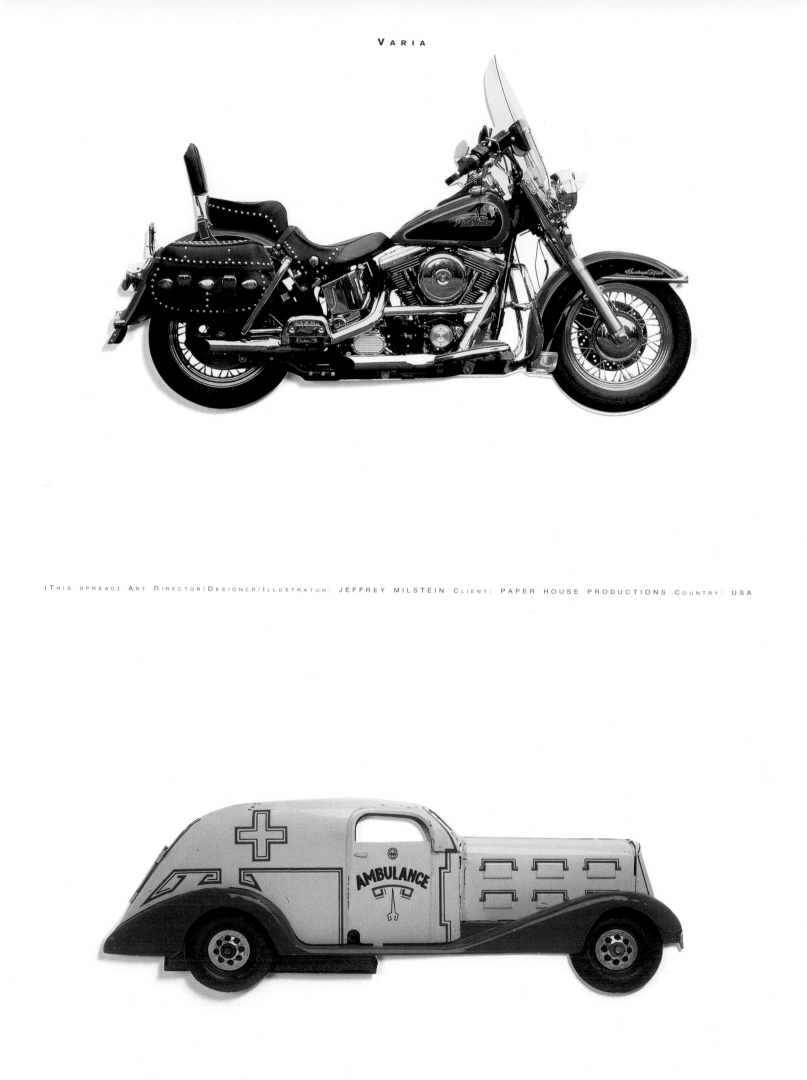

(This spread) Art Director/Designer/Illustrator: JEFFREY MILSTEIN Client: PAPER HOUSE PRODUCTIONS Country: USA

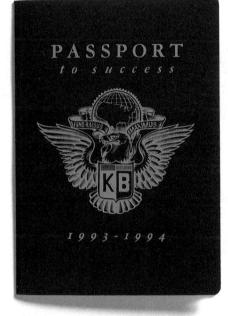

The President of
Kathryn Beich, Inc.
hereby requests all whom
it may concern to permit
the citizen named herein
to pass without delay
or hindrance down
the road to success.

PASSPORT
to success

KB

1993 - 1994

Grand Prize

If you earn the greatest number of miles during the course of the program (and your total net sales have increased over last year) you will receive this incredible prize.

DREAM VACATION

Imagine a five-day getaway to a luxurious resort in Arizona next winter. Or maybe a trip to Washington D.C. is more to your liking with historic monuments and fascinating museums. Of course if you want to breathe some clean mountain air you could head north for a five-day adventure in the Canadian Rockies. Perhaps you'd like to explore the world of fine dining during a five-night stay in San Francisco. How about a Caribbean cruise aboard the incredible Nordic Empress? You could even spend time south of the border on a fun in the sun trip to the sparkling beaches of Cancun, Mexico. These are just some examples of how you could spend your dream vacation fund – it's up to you to decide where and when you want to go!

20

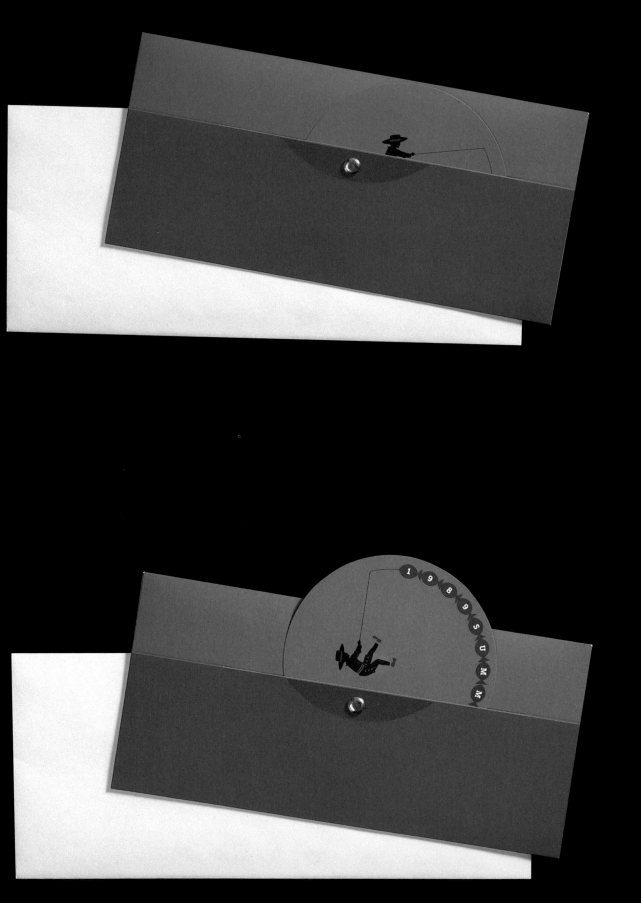

(PRECEDING SPREAD LEFT) ART DIRECTOR/DESIGNER: BRUCE EDWARDS ILLUSTRATOR: JAKE AGENCY: RAPP COLLINS COMMUNICATIONS CLIENT: KATHRYN BEICH (NESTLE-BEICH'S FUNDRAISING) COUNTRY: USA □ (PRECEDING SPREAD RIGHT) ART DIRECTOR: GARRY EMERY DESIGNER/AGENCY: EMERY VINCENT ASSOC. CLIENT: CARMEN FURNITURE (SALES) PTY LIMITED COUNTRY: AUSTRALIA □ (OPPOSITE PAGE) ART DIRECTOR/DESIGNER/ILLUSTRATOR: KEISUKE UNOSAWA AGENCY/CLIENT: KEISUKE UNOSAWA DESIGN COUNTRY: JAPAN □ (THIS PAGE) ART DIRECTOR/DESIGNER: KEN HERNDON PHOTOGRAPHER: JOSEPH HUMPHREY AGENCY: KEN HERNDON GRAPHIC DESIGN CLIENT: IMAGES HAIR SALON COUNTRY: USA

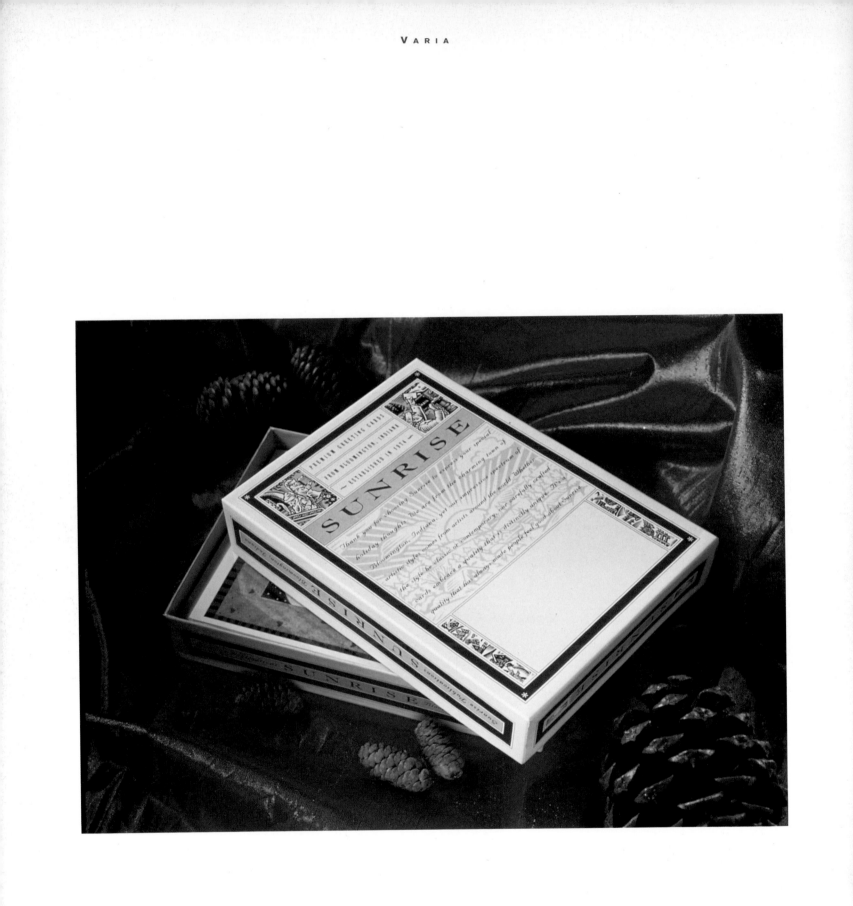

(ABOVE) ART DIRECTOR/DESIGNER: SCOTT MIRES PHOTOGRAPHER: CARL VANDERSCHUIT ILLUSTRATOR: TRACY SABIN AGENCY:
MIRES DESIGN COUNTRY: USA □ (OPPOSITE) ART DIRECTOR/DESIGNER/ILLUSTRATOR/AGENCY: SHIGERU AKIZUKI COUNTRY: JAPAN

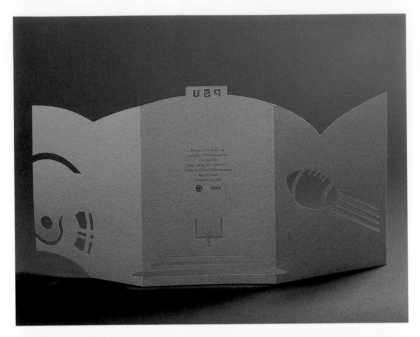

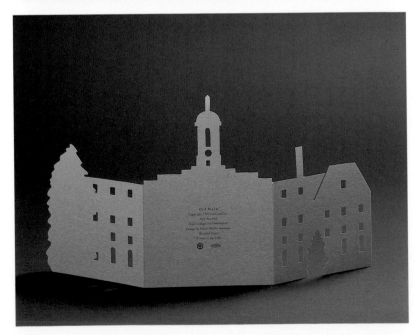

(OPPOSITE PAGE) ART DIRECTOR: KRISTIN SOMMESE DESIGNER: KRISTIN SOMMESE AGENCY: SOMMESE DESIGN CLIENT: CUTCARDS INC. COUNTRY: USA □ (THIS PAGE) ART DIRECTOR/DESIGNER: XIAO YONG CLIENT: YÉ DESIGN COUNTRY: CHINA □ (FOLLOWING PAGE) ART DIRECTOR: SEYMOUR CHWAST DESIGNER: SEYMOUR CHWAST ILLUSTRATORS: R. KENTON NELSON, ROBERT CRAWFORD, LOU BEACH, DAVE JONASON DESIGN FIRM: THE PUSHPIN GROUP CLIENT: THE PUSHPIN ASSOCIATES COUNTRY: USA □ (PAGE 224) ART DIRECTOR: ISABELLE PAQUIN DESIGNER: JEAN-FRANÇOIS COUVIGNOU ILLUSTRATOR: FRÉDÉRIC EIBNER AGENCY: SUN COMMUNICATIONS DESIGN CLIENT: DOMTAR SPECIALTY FINE PAPERS COUNTRY: CANADA

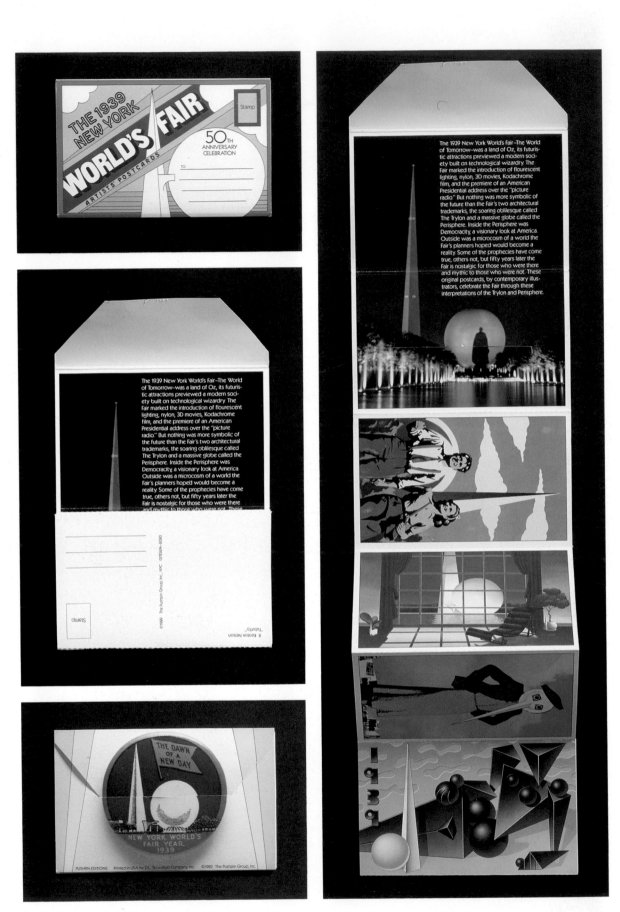

INDEX

VERZEICHNIS

INDEX

ABELSON, DANNY NEW YORK, NY 212 421 5888 99

ADAMSON, MARK-STEEN LONDON, GREAT BRITAIN 071 722 1113 129

AHLERS, SUSANNE MUNICH, GERMANY 089 222 801 107

AITCHISON, JIM SINGAPORE 0322 0448 94

AKIZUKI, SHIGERU TOKYO, JAPAN 03 3412 1371...............................203

ANDERSON, CHARLES S. MINNEAPOLIS, MN 612 339 5181.........72, 79, 88,
....109, 135

ANDERSON, CHUCK MINNEAPOLIS, MN 612 339 3247 87

ANGELI, PRIMO SAN FRANCISCO, CA 415 974 6100 66

ASHBY, NEAL ANNAPOLIS, MD 410 263 4983 167

BACCARI, ALBERTO TORINO, ITALY 011 881 0111 146

BAILEY, CRAIG SAN FRANCISCO, CA 415 543 6548 ....54, 121

BARONET, WILLIE DALLAS, TX 214 954 0316 ....26, 185

BAUER, MICHAELA GRÜNWALD, GERMANY 089 641 0094..............58, 162

BAUR, RUEDI MONTREUIL, FRANCE 01 4988 8050 ....29, 152, 182

BBV/MICHAEL BAVIERA ZURICH, SWITZERLAND 01 251 1755 120,
....146, 147, 195

BECKMANN, ANDREAS DÜSSELDORF, GERMANY 0211 130 010...........38, 39

BENES, PAVEL PRAGUE, CZECH REPUBLIC 02 537 8083 ....116, 180

BIRCHLER, KARIN SWITZERLAND...87

BITTER, PETER R. HEIDELBERG, GERMANY 06221 484 456 31

BLECHMAN, R.O. NEW YORK, NY 212 869 1630 55

BORGSTÄDT, BARBARA BENDESTORF, GERMANY 04183 6123 65

BOSSER, FRÉDÉRIC PARIS, FRANCE 01 4770 8136 125

BRADLEY, MARK INDIANAPOLIS, IN 317 264 8000 91

BREIER, LO HAMBURG, GERMANY 040 448 040-0 ....65, 144

BROCK, MICHAEL LOS ANGELES, CA 213 932 0283 ....45, 48, 56

BROCKBANK, LYNDA LONDON, GREAT BRITAIN 071 607 6733 49

BROOKS, ALAN NEW YORK, NY 212 689 3620 30

BUCHANAN, CANDACE DALLAS, TX 214 522 7273 193

CALDWELL, SUSAN WILTON, CT 203 834 1885 4

CAMPBELL, MIKE PHOENIX, AZ 602 955 2707 30

CANTOR, MARK MIAMI, FL 305 854 1000 ....90, 91

CARPENTER, POLLY NEW YORK, NY 212 431 6666 2

CARRUTHERS, ROY BROOKLYN, NY 718 965 1330 193

CARTER, DAVID DALLAS, TX 214 826 4631 49

CEHOVIN, EDUARD LJUBLJANA, SLOVENIA 62, 108

CHAN, ALAN HONG KONG 0527 8228 ....135, 138, 139

CHIAO, CARY SAN FRANCISCO, CA 415 861 1128............................104

CHONG TAM, JULIA PALOS VERDES, CA 310 378 7583 ....60, 64

CHWAST, SEYMOUR NEW YORK, NY 212 674 8080 ....40, 206

CLARK, JOHN LOS ANGELES, CA 213 226 1086 77

CLARK, JOHN PROVIDENCE, RI 401 521 4678 25

CLEAVER, PHIL LONDON, GREAT BRITAIN 081 566 2807 194

COOK, ROGER PRINCETON, NJ 609 452 1666 37

CORNERSTONE STAFF NEW YORK, NY 212 686 6046 156

COSTARELLA, VITTORIO SEATTLE, WA 206 282 8857 82

COSTELLO, SAL KANSAS CITY, MO 816 531 1992 101

COUVIGNOU, JEAN-FRANÇOIS MONTREAL, CANADA 514 521 5464 224

COVERDALE, JAC MINNEAPOLIS, MN 612 339 3902 140

DABERKO, TRACI SEATTLE, WA 206 624 0551 123

DANKL, HERIBERT SALZBURG, AUSTRIA 0662 824 206...................140

DENNARD, BOB DALLAS, TX 214 233 0430 36

DITKO, STEVE PHOENIX, AZ 602 955 2707 30

DORST, MARIE-LUISE MUNICH, GERMANY 089 346 861 138

DUFFETT, CAROL VLAEBERG, SOUTH AFRICA 021 419 9292..............189

EDWARDS, BRUCE MINNEAPOLIS, MN 612 373 3000 ....78, 198

EISELEIN, MARTINA DÜSSELDORF, GERMANY 0211 674 826 68

EMERY VINCENT ASSOCIATES MELBOURNE, AUSTRALIA 03 699 3822.........53,
....71, 199

EMERY, GARRY MELBOURNE, AUSTRALIA 03 699 3822 ....53, 71, 199

ERBER, DENNIS INDIANAPOLIS, IN 317 587 3027 135

ERICKSON-SIKORA, LYNETTE MINNEAPOLIS, MN 612 338 4462 100

FABRIZIO, STEVEN NEW YORK, NY 212 421 5888 99

FALKNER, ERICH VIENNA, AUSTRIA 01 940 505 136

FASICK-JONES, SUSAN CHESTER, CT 203 526 9597 153

FELDER, PETER RANKWEIL, AUSTRIA 05522 415 10-20 97

FLORES, TUNA NEW YORK, NY 212 620 0506 191

FLYNN, DANIEL MICHAEL ALBUQUERQUE, NM 505 243 4000 ......84, 87

FORSTNER, MATHIAS GAUTING, GERMANY 089 850 6998 52

FOWLER, THOMAS G. STAMFORD, CT 203 329 1105 ....83, 96, 137, 154

FULLER, JOEL MIAMI, FL 305 854 1000 ....90, 91

GAIS, MICHAEL DÜSSELDORF, GERMANY 0211 393 423 93

GATES, GUILBERT NEW YORK, NY 212 475 2390 124

GAY, CLIVE H. TRANSVAAL, SOUTH AFRICA 011 472 3642 73

GHIELMETTI, PHILIPPE PARIS, FRANCE 01 4321 8401............46, 95, 115

GIBBS, STEVE DALLAS, TX 214 954 0316 ....26, 185

GIRARDIN, MICHEL ZURICH, SWITZERLAND 144

GOOD, PETER CHESTER, CT 203 526 9597 153

GORMAN, PAT NEW YORK, NY 212 620 0506 191

GRAY, COLIN GLASGOW, GREAT BRITAIN 041 334 4020 171

HAAG, BRUNO STUTTGART, GERMANY 0711 649 1215 41

HAGENBUCHER, THOMAS DÜSSELDORF, GERMANY 0211 782 142 ....48, 93

HALBACH, THEKLA DÜSSELDORF, GERMANY 0211 782 142 ....48, 93

HAMBLY, BOB TORONTO, CANADA 416 504 2742 ....57, 172

HARTZ, DANIEL KASTORF, GERMANY 04501 1680 145

HARTZ, FRANZISKA KASTORF, GERMANY 04501 1680..............145, 178

HASLINGER, WOLFGANG KLOSTERNEUBURG, AUSTRIA 02243 886 71........26,
..................................50, 62, 81, 83, 107, 140, 173, 187

HAUSWIRTH, TODD MINNEAPOLIS, MN 612 339 5181.........72, 88, 109

HECK, MATT AUSTIN, TX 512 477 0050 67

HEINE, DIRK GARBSEN, GERMANY 05137 134 17 164

HENSCHKE, THOMAS STUTTGART, GERMANY 0711 649 1215 41

HERNDON, KEN LOUISVILLE, KY 502 451 6413 201

HEYMANN, MONICA USA 165

HICKMANN, FONS M. DÜSSELDORF, GERMANY 0211 494 730 92

HICKS, MIKE AUSTIN, TX 512 477 0050 67

HILL, RANDALL DALLAS, TX 214 826 4631 49

HINRICHS, KIT SAN FRANCISCO, CA 415 981 6612 111

HINSHAW, MICHAEL LARKSPUR, CA 415 925 3300......................80

HIVELY, CHARLES HOUSTON, TX 713 961 2888 ....74, 128

HO NGAI SING, JOYCE HONG KONG 0574 8399 21

HOI, TRACY HONG KONG 0526 6991 157

HOLDEMAN, BRUCE DENVER, CO 303 825 7913 185

HOLLOWAY, CHRISTO NEW YORK, NY 212 431 8996 ....93, 131

HOOVER, CAROL LARKSPUR, CA 415 925 3300 80

HOWART, PAUL MINNEAPOLIS, MN 612 339 5181 ....109, 135

HOYNE, ANDREW MELBOURNE, AUSTRALIA 03 690 6458 170

HUBNER, JULIE NEW YORK, NY 212 645 7858 132

HUNTER, KENT NEW YORK, NY 212 421 5888 99

JACOBS, BYRON HONG KONG 0526 6991 ....61, 157

JACOBS, JOHAN GROOT-BIJGAARDEN, BELGIUM 02 466 5641 83

JANSEN, HEIKE FRANKFURT/M., GERMANY 069 789 08-412 106

JINEL, STEVEN PARIS, FRANCE 01 4770 8136 125

JOHNSON NEWHOUSE, META DALLAS, TX 214 954 0316 26

JOHNSON, MARK MINNEAPOLIS, MN 612 332 2445 143

JOHNSON, SCOTT ROCKFORD, IL 815 229 0931 63

JORGENSEN, GRANT ADELAIDE, AUSTRALIA 08 271 7753 83

JOSEPH, STEVEN SYDNEY, AUSTRALIA 02 360 6755 22

KAGAROV, ERKEN MOSCOW, RUSSIA 095 235 0949 155

KAJABA, THOMAS AUSTRIA 42, 43

KARLSSON, KENNETH STOCKHOLM, SWEDEN 08 301 502 ....53, 151

KASPER, INES OSNABRÜCK, GERMANY 0541 260 059 81

KENDALL, DEWITT CHICAGO, IL 312 275 7884 44

KHAI MENG, THAM SINGAPORE 0322 0448 133

KIM, DOO H. SEOUL, KOREA 02 785 7599 ......151, 158, 159, 163

KIMBALL, KELLYE DALLAS, TX 214 954 0316 ....26, 185

KIMURA, NIO OSAKA, JAPAN 06 535 1136 ....102, 103, 184

KNOBEL, URS J. BAAR, SWITZERLAND 042 323 150 87

KOHLA, HANS EASTWOOD, AUSTRALIA 08 373 0616 85

KRAEGE, KLAUS HAMBURG, GERMANY 040 870 3175 151

KRALL, TERRY MILWAUKEE, WI 414 224 0212 142

KRUSE, JANET SEATTLE, WA 206 624 0551 123

KUO, SAM NEW YORK, NY 212 343 9212 104

KYRAL, VERONIKA VIENNA, AUSTRIA 01 545 7174 ....108, 110

LANGKAFEL, GERD BERLIN, GERMANY 030 469 0090 177

LARAMORE, JEFF INDIANAPOLIS, IN 317 264 8000 91

LARSON, JEFF ROCKFORD, IL 815 229 0931 63

LECLERC, BERNIE USA 70

LEE, DONGIL SEOUL, KOREA 02 785 7599 ....151, 158, 159, 163

LEE, SEUNG HEE SEOUL, KOREA 02 785 7599 ....158, 159

LELAND, RON USA 169

LEONG, SZE TSUNG PASADENA, CA 818 584 5191 110

LERCH, DAVID HOUSTON, TX 713 963 8607 47

LEUNG, JAMES WAI MO BROOKLYN, NY 718 836 4695 107

LÉVY, JEAN-BENOIT BASEL, SWITZERLAND 061 271 2571 160

LEY, MAX BERLIN, GERMANY 030 469 0090 177

LIU, MAY NEW YORK, NY 212 925 3372 134

LO, PETER HONG KONG 0527 8228 135

LOGVIN, ANDREY MOSCOW, RUSSIA 095 942 8143 176

LOVEN, PAUL PHOENIX, AZ 602 253 0335 169

MACINDOE, BRUCE MINNEAPOLIS, MN 612 338 4462 100

MANDEL, RACHEL USA 135

MARSCHALL, MICHAEL FRANKFURT/M., GERMANY 069 789 08-412 106

MARUYAMA, KARL S. STAMFORD, CT 203 329 1105 137

MASTERS, ANNE WASHINGTON, DC 202 337 3748 27

MATSUMOTO, TAKAAKI NEW YORK, NY 212 807 0248 ....92, 106, 117

MCEVOY, VINCENT LONDON, GREAT BRITAIN 071 485 4043 113

MCFARLAND, AMY LOS ANGELES, CA 213 857 6588 119

MCGINN, MICHAEL NEW YORK, NY 212 807 0248 ....92, 106, 117

MCPHERSON, MICHAEL WATERTOWN, MA 617 924 6050 112

MEINECKE, KURT CHICAGO, IL 312 787 4504 87

MENDEZ, REBECA PASADENA, CA 818 584 5191 110

MENZE, LUTZ WUPPERTAL, GERMANY 0202 318 824 98

MERTEN, BARRY A. DENVER, CO 303 322 1451 79

MEYER, KARIN OSNABRÜCK, GERMANY 0541 940 0400 161

MIEDANER, ANDREAS HAMBURG, GERMANY 040 448 040-0 65

MILSTEIN, JEFF WOODSTOCK, NY 914 679 8403 ....34, 35, 196, 197

MIRES, SCOTT SAN DIEGO, CA 619 234 6631 202

MORGAN, GREG DALLAS, TX 214 522 7273 193

MORLA, JENNIFER SAN FRANCISCO, CA 415 543 6548 ....54, 121

MOUSNER, JIM HOUSTON, TX 713 523 5119 83

MULLER, JOHN KANSAS CITY, MO 816 531 1992 101

MÜLLER, DAGMAR DÜSSELDORF, GERMANY 0211 130 010 ....39, 30

MÜLLER, IRENE STUTTGART, GERMANY 0711 567 057 28

MURRAY, KAREN WELLINGTON, NEW ZEALAND 04 384 6164 83

NEWELL, FRANCES LONDON, GREAT BRITAIN 071 722 1113 129

NOERBAMBANG, EDWIN M. BANDUNG, INDONESIA 022 250 0295 194

OEVERMANN, STEFAN LANDSBERG, GERMANY 08191 210 99 138

OLSON, DANIEL MINNEAPOLIS, MN 612 333 2809 79

OTTE, THOMAS OSNABRÜCK, GERMANY 0541 258 859 81

OUDIN, JÉROME PARIS, FRANCE 01 4285 2063 108

PALMER, RANDY USA 169

PALMQVIST, JEANETTE BORAS, SWEDEN 033 114 441 51

PALMQVIST, KARI BORAS, SWEDEN 033 114 441 51

PAQUIN, ISABELLE MONTREAL, CANADA 514 521 5464 224

PARHAM, JOHN NEW YORK, NY 212 645 7501 65

PETEET, REX DALLAS, TX 214 761 9400 114

PETRICK, ROBERT CHICAGO, IL 312 486 2880 105

PIERCY, CLIVE LOS ANGELES, CA 175

PITALLO, PIER PAOLO MILAN, ITALY 02 4801 2762 56

PLAKOLM, GERHARD AUSTRIA 42, 43

POTH, TOM AUSTIN, TX 512 477 0050 67

PUTTAERT, HUGO GROOT-BIJGAARDEN, BELGIUM 02 466 5641 83

QUADENS, POL GROOT-BIJGAARDEN, BELGIUM 02 466 5641 83

RAYE, ROBYNNE SEATTLE, WA 206 282 8857 82

REDMAN, ANTONY SINGAPORE 0322 0448 133

REGAN, NICKY GLASGOW, GREAT BRITAIN 041 334 4020 171

RENK, THOMAS INDIANAPOLIS, IN 317 587 3027 135

RENNER, SABINE WALDSTETTEN, GERMANY 07171 442 54 126

RESS, LAURA CHICAGO, IL 312 486 2880 105

RICKABAUGH, ERIC GAHANNA, OH 614 337 2229 45

RIOS, FRANCISCO HOUSTON, TX 713 523 5119 83
ROMAGNOLI, MARIA CRISTINA ROMA, ITALY 06 8621 8260 59
ROMANO, ANTONIO ROMA, ITALY 06 841 3001 ....108, 150
ROSS, JIM INDIANAPOLIS, IN 317 921 9753 118
ROTHWELL, MERCEDES CANADA 166, 172
ROTMAN, SARA NEW YORK, NY 212 833 7244 99
ROWAN, COLIN JAMES SYDNEY, AUSTRALIA 112

SABIN, TRACY SAN DIEGO, CA 619 484 8712 135
SAINT-LOUBERT BIÉ, JÉROME PARIS, FRANCE 01 4462 9171 ....19, 148, 174
SAMATA, GREG DUNDEE, IL 708 428 8600 24
SAMATA, PAT DUNDEE, IL 708 428 8600 24
SANTANA, MARUCHI NEW YORK, NY 212 645 7501 65
SAYLES, JOHN DES MOINES, IA 515 243 2922 23
SCHAFER, VICKIE BALTIMORE, MD 410 467 7300 130
SCHEURER, JÜRG HAMBURG, GERMANY 040 448 040-0 144
SCHEWE, JOSEF HAMBURG, GERMANY 040 410 7561 76
SCHIRMER, HEIKE DÜSSELDORF, GERMANY 0211 498 2034 68
SCHNEIDER, ROLAND GRÜNWALD, GERMANY 089 641 0093 ......58, 147, 162
SCHNEIDMAN, JARED NEW YORK, NY 212 475 2390 124
SCHROEBLER, DAGMAR AICHACH, GERMANY 108
SELFE, MARK SAN FRANCISCO, CA 415 981 6612 111
SERRANO, JOSE SAN DIEGO, CA 619 234 6631 ....64, 79
SHANNON, SUSANNA PARIS, FRANCE 01 4285 2063 ....19, 108, 148, 174
SHEK, MICHELLE HONG KONG 0526 6991 61
SHIMIZU, MASAYUKI OSAKA, JAPAN 06 535 1136 ....102, 103, 184
SHIN, JIWON SEOUL, KOREA 02 785 7599 ....151, 158, 159, 163
SIEGER DESIGN SASSENBERG, GERMANY 05426 9492-0 18
SIEGER, MICHAEL SASSENBERG, GERMANY 05426 9492-0 18
SIKORA, STEVEN MINNEAPOLIS, MN 612 338 4462 100
SIMPSON, GREG NEW YORK, NY 212 598 9111 40
SKJEI, MICHAEL MINNEAPOLIS, MN 612 374 3528 32
SKOVLUND, CARSTEN HERNING, DENMARK 09721 4000 53
SMITH, MICHAEL GAHANNA, OH 614 337 2229 45
SOFFIANTINO, TITTI TORINO, ITALY 011 881 0111 146
SOMMESE, KRISTIN STATE COLLEGE, PA 814 238 7484 204
SORRELL, JOHN LONDON, GREAT BRITAIN 071 722 1113 129
SPATCHURST, JOHN SYDNEY, AUSTRALIA 02 360 6755 112
SPEER, LESLIE WALDSTETTEN, GERMANY 07171 442 54 126
STEIMEL, KEITH NEW YORK, NY 212 686 6046 156
STOFFREGEN, CORNELIA HAMBURG, GERMANY 040 899 1205 76
STONE, GINA NEW YORK, NY 212 421 5888 99
STRASSBURGER, MICHAEL SEATTLE, WA 206 282 8857 82
STUTZ, RALF OFFENBACH, GERMANY 069 816 161 86
SWIETER, JOHN DALLAS, TX 214 720 6020 137

TAI-KEUNG, KAN HONG KONG 0574 8399 21
TARTAKOVER, DAVID TEL-AVIV, ISRAEL 03 517 3745 69

TEMPLIN, JOEL MINNEAPOLIS, MN 612 339 5181 ....109, 183
THOMAS, ANDREW LONDON, GREAT BRITAIN 071 388 5832 ....20, 60
TILK, ANDREA HAMBURG, GERMANY 28
TOLLESON, STEVE SAN FRANCISCO, CA 415 626 7796 127
TRAPP, DOUG MINNEAPOLIS, MN 612 332 3993 104
TRICKETT, LYNN LONDON, GREAT BRITAIN 071 388 5832 ....20, 60
TSOI, CHEN SHUN HONG KONG 0527 8228 ....138, 139
TUCKER, BARRIE EASTWOOD, AUSTRALIA 08 373 0616 ....73, 85, 87

UHLMANN, MONIKA WARTHAUSEN, GERMANY 07351 7805 74
ULMAJA, NINA STOCKHOLM, SWEDEN 08 612 7271 190
ULTIMO, CLARE NEW YORK, NY 212 645 7858 132
UNOSAWA, KEISUKE TOKYO, JAPAN 03 5430 2154 ....65, 68, 76, 122,
....149, 188, 192, 200
UTIKAL, IRIS DÜSSELDORF, GERMANY 0211 393 423 93

VAN OMMEN, CARL HAMBURG, GERMANY 040 448 040-0 65
VANCE, BILL DALLAS, TX 214 954 0316 185
VARASCHINI, LUCA MILAN, ITALY 02 5519 1109 186
VAUGHN, RICK ALBUQUERQUE, NM 505 243 4000 ....84, 87
VON RENNER, IVO HAMBURG, GERMANY 040 491 7096 31

WALLIS, TIM MILWAUKEE, WI 414 224 0212 142
WATERBURY, TODD PORTLAND, OR 503 228 4381 70
WEBB, BRIAN LONDON, GREAT BRITAIN 071 388 5832 ....20, 60
WEDEEN, STEVE ALBUQUERQUE, NM 505 243 4000 ....84, 141
WEIHS, SASCHA BIBERACH, GERMANY 07351 173 43 ....149, 181, 192
WEITZ, CARTER LINCOLN, NE 402 475 2800 89
WELCH, DEREK DALLAS, TX 214 761 9400 114
WERNER, SHARON MINNEAPOLIS, MN 612 338 2550 ....70, 75
WIEMER, UTE OSNABRÜCK, GERMANY 0541 940 0400 161
WIESE, BRUNO K. HAMBURG, GERMANY 040 603 8982 ....33, 155
WINN, MARK SAN FRANCISCO, CA 415 626 7796 127
WONG, EDDIE SINGAPORE 0322 0448 94
WONG, VALERIE SAN FRANCISCO, CA 415 861 1128 104
WOOLLEY, BARBARA TORONTO, CANADA 416 504 2742 ....57, 172
WURSTER, FRITZ W. WALDSTETTEN, GERMANY 07171 442 54 126

YANG SEAH, SIM SINGAPORE 0322 0448 94
YANG, JIMMY LONDON, GREAT BRITAIN 071 221 9900 147
YONG, XIAO HELSINKI, FINLAND 205
YOUNG, DAVID INDIANAPOLIS, IN 317 264 8000 91
YOUNG, ROSE DENDY VLAEBERG, SOUTH AFRICA 021 419 9292 189
YU CHI KONG, EDDY HONG KONG 0574 8399 21

(Z)OO PRODUKTIES, ANITA STEKETTE DEN HAAG, NETHERLANDS 070 364 2309 83

AKIZUKI, SHIGERU TOKYO, JAPAN 03 3412 1371 203

ANDERSON, CHARLES S. MINNEAPOLIS, MN 612 339 5181 135

ANGERER, BERNHARD VIENNA, AUSTRIA 01 533 6118 ....42, 43

ASHBY, NEAL ANNAPOLIS, MD 410 263 4983 167

BARRY, LINDA USA 191

BAUER, MICHAELA GRÜNWALD, GERMANY 089 641 0094 147

BBV/MICHAEL BAVIERA ZURICH, SWITZERLAND 01 251 1755 120,

....146, 147, 195

BEACH, LOU USA 206

BENINCASA, MARISSA USA 30

BITTER, PETER R. HEIDELBERG, GERMANY 06221 484 456 31

BLACKBURN, ROB MELBOURNE, AUSTRALIA 03 690 0733 170

BROOKS, ALAN NEW YORK, NY 212 689 3620 30

BROOKS, HEATHER EDISON, NJ 30

BRUNO NEW YORK, NY 212 645 9588 165

BURDA, RICK USA 131

CANNON, BILL (PAT HACKETT, USA 206 447 1600) 123

CARRUTHERS, ROY BROOKLYN, NY 718 965 1330 193

CHONG TAM, JULIA PALOS VERDES, CA 310 378 7583 ....60, 64

CLARK, JOHN PROVIDENCE, RI 401 521 4678 25

COBURN, MARSHA USA 49

COMBS, JONATHAN (PAT HACKETT, USA 206 447 1600) 123

COOK, ROGER PRINCETON, NJ 609 452 1666 37

COSMO-TONE GERMANY 74

COUSIN, STÉFANIE ZURICH, SWITZERLAND 144

CRACKNEL, ALAN HONG KONG 138, 139

CRAWFORD, ROBERT USA 206

CSA ARCHIVE MINNEAPOLIS, MN 612 339 1263 ....72, 88

CULVER, W.C. CZECH REPUBLIC 116

CURTIS, STEVE USA 101

CZERNY, PETER AUSTRIA 42, 43

D'ALTAN, PAOLO MILAN, ITALY 02 4801 2762 56

DENNARD, BOB DALLAS, TX 214 233 0430 36

DUCHAINE, RANDY NEW YORK, NY 212 243 4371 137

EAGER, DARRELL MINNEAPOLIS, MN 612 333 8732 ....72, 88, 109

EDELMAN, TEDDY HAWLEYVILLE, CT 134

EIBNER, FRÉDÉRIC OUTREMONT, CANADA 514 272 4798 224

EMERY VINCENT ASSOCIATES MELBOURNE, AUSTRALIA 03 699 3822 112

EYNON, DAVID L. USA 37

FADDA, GIUSEPPE MARIA ROME, ITALY 06 275 4574 ....108, 150

FANCELLO, ANTONIO MILAN, ITALY 02 404 9022 186

FEILER, TOM TORONTO, CANADA 416 929 0071 166

FLYNN, DANIEL MICHAEL ALBUQUERQUE, NM 505 243 4000 87

FOWLER, THOMAS G. STAMFORD, CT 203 329 1105 96

GABERSCEK, BORIS LJUBLJANA, SLOVENIA 62

GATES, GUILBERT NEW YORK, NY 212 475 2390 124

GERHOLD, BILL USA 84

GOOD, PETER CHESTER, CT 203 526 9597 153

GRAY, COLIN GLASGOW, GREAT BRITAIN 041 334 4020 171

GRITZBACH, WERNER HAMBURG, GERMANY 040 249 002 168

HAAG, BRUNO STUTTGART, GERMANY 0711 649 1215 41

HARTO, DAVID (PAT HACKETT, USA 206 447 1600) 123

HARTZ, DANIEL KASTORF, GERMANY 04501 1680 178

HARTZ, WERNER STUTTGART, GERMANY 145

HASLINGER, WOLFGANG KLOSTERNEUBURG, AUSTRIA 02243 886 71 ....

....62, 107, 173

HEFFERNAN, TERRY SAN FRANCISCO, CA 415 626 1999 2

HEUKAMP, CICO WUPPERTAL, GERMANY 0202 403 572 98

HINRICHS, KIT SAN FRANCISCO, CA 415 981 6612 111

HOCHSTÖGER, ANDREAS VIENNA, AUSTRIA 01 940 505 136

HOFFMANN, KONRAD MITTELBIBERACH, GERMANY 07351 291 57 74

HÖNICKE, ERHARD BASEL, SWITZERLAND 061 261 6894 125

HORNUNG, DIETMAR DÜSSELDORF, GERMANY 0211 631 815 68

HOWART, PAUL MINNEAPOLIS, MN 612 339 5181 135

HUMPHREY, JOSEPH USA 201

IRMITER, PAUL MINNEAPOLIS, MN 612 870 9007 ....79, 88

JAKE USA 198

JONASON, DAVE USA 206

KAGAROV, ERKEN MOSCOW, RUSSIA 095 235 0949 155

KAPLAN, CAROL, STUDIO BOSTON, MA 617 426 1131 130

KARLSSON, KENNETH STOCKHOLM, SWEDEN 08 301 502 ......53, 151

KATIMS, KATHLEEN NEW YORK, NY 212 475 2390 124

KELLER, TOM LOS ANGELES, CA 213 934 2822 ....45, 56

KLEIN + WILSON DALLAS, TX 214 747 1714 49

KOCH, MITCH USA 09

KRAEGE, KLAUS HAMBURG, GERMANY 040 870 3175 151

KYRAL, VERONIKA VIENNA, AUSTRIA 01 545 7174 110

LANDECKER, TOM SAN FRANCISCO, CA 415 864 8888 104

LANDWEHR, CLAUDIA OSNABRÜCK, GERMANY 0541 258 859 81

LARSON, JEFF ROCKFORD, IL 815 229 0931 63

LEBER, PAUL ZURICH, SWITZERLAND 01 252 1652 179

LERCH, DAVID HOUSTON, TX 713 963 8607 47

LERCH, LISA HOUSTON, TX 713 963 8607 47

LESMONO, HENDRA JAKARTA, INDONESIA 194
LÉVY, JEAN-BENOIT BASEL, SWITZERLAND 061 271 2571 160
LIMINTON, ROGER AUSTRALIA 83
LOGVIN, ANDREY MOSCOW, RUSSIA 095 942 8143 176
LOVEN, PAUL PHOENIX, AZ 602 253 0335 23
LYONS, WENDY USA 23
LYTER, BARBARA LOS ANGELES, CA 213 857 6588 119

MCPHERSON, MICHAEL WATERTOWN, MA 617 924 6050 112
MEISSNER, ROLAND BUCCLEAUCH, SOUTH AFRICA 011 802 1538 73
MILLER, JULES MILWAUKEE, WI 414 224 0212 142
MILSTEIN, JEFF WOODSTOCK, NY 914 679 8403 . . . . 34, 35, 196, 197
MIRES DESIGN STAFF SAN DIEGO, CA 619 234 6631 64
MITCHELL, CORINNE MINNEAPOLIS, MN 104
MONGE, MARIO ITALY 146
MYERS, BARRY SILVER SPRING, MD 301 585 8617 167

NAIM, NAD LONDON, GREAT BRITAIN 071 624 1874 147
NELEMAN, HANS NEW YORK, NY 212 274 1000 99
NELSON, R. KENTON USA 206
NIELSON, HENRIETTE AARHUS, DENMARK 179
NISIKAWA, KATUZI JAPAN 102, 103
NORBERG, MARC MINNEAPOLIS, MN 612 340 9863 24

OCHSLER, UWE BENDESTORF, GERMANY 04183 6123 65
OGILVIE, ALISTAIR GREAT BRITAIN 113

PALMQVIST, KARI BORAS, SWEDEN 033 114 4441 51
PEAK, ROBERT ORLANDO, FL 407 661 4096 48
PETEET, REX DALLAS, TX 214 761 9400 114
PPA DESIGN LIMITED HONG KONG 0526 6991 . . . . 61, 157

RAY, MAN 121
REINHOLD, FRIEDRUN HAMBURG, GERMANY 040 420 9118 76
ROBERT, FRANÇOIS CHICAGO, IL 312 787 0777 105
ROBINSON, BARRY USA 111
RONCHI, ANNA MILAN, ITALY 186

SABIN, TRACY SAN DIEGO, CA 619 484 8712 . . . . 79, 135, 202
SAINT-LOUBERT BIÉ, JÉROME PARIS, FRANCE 01 4462 9171 148

SANTANA, MARUCHI NEW YORK, NY 212 645 7501 65
SCHELS, WALTER HAMBURG, GERMANY 040 850 4646 138
SCHNEIDMAN, JARED NEW YORK, NY 212 475 2390 124
SCHROEDER, MIKE DALLAS, TX 214 761 9400 114
SCHULTE, LYNN MINNEAPOLIS, MN 612 339 3247 . . . . 70, 87
SCHWAB, MICHAEL SAUSALITO, CA 415 331 7621 78
SETH TORONTO, CANADA 416 927 1104 172
SILPOCH, JAN CZECH REPUBLIC 116
SINKLER, PAUL MINNEAPOLIS, MN 612 343 0325 183
SKOVLUND, CARSTEN HERNING, DENMARK 09721 4000 53
SMITH, MICHAEL GAHANNA, OH 614 337 2229 45
STERNBACH, SCOTT USA 40
STEWART, DOUG USA 79
STINGLEY, JOHN MINNEAPOLIS, MN 612 332 2445 143

TAMMEN, ROLF OSNABRÜCK, GERMANY 0541 940 0400 161
TEMPLIN, JOEL MINNEAPOLIS, MN 612 339 5181 183
TRICKETT & WEBB LIMITED LONDON, GREAT BRITAIN 071 388 5832 . . . . 20, 60

ULTIMO, CLARE NEW YORK, NY 212 645 7858 132
UNOSAWA, KEISUKE TOKYO, JAPAN 03 5430 2154 . . . . 188, 200

VANDERSCHUIT, CARL USA 79, 202
VON RENNER, IVO HAMBURG, GERMANY 040 491 7096 31

WALLIS, TIM MILWAUKEE, WI 414 224 0212 142
WATERBURY, TODD PORTLAND, OR 503 228 4381 70
WEDEEN, STEVE ALBUQUERQUE, NM 505 243 4000 141
WEIHS, SASCHA BIBERACH, GERMANY 07351 173 43 . . . . 181, 192
WEISS, MAX ST. MORITZ, SWITZERLAND 137
WELCH, DEREK DALLAS, TX 214 761 9400 114
WERLEIN, JENS WALDSTETTEN, GERMANY 07171 442 54 126
WERNER, SHARON MINNEAPOLIS, MN 612 338 2550 70
WINES, BRAD USA 36
WOBER, THOMAS GERMANY 138
WURSTER, FRITZ W. WALDSTETTEN, GERMANY 07171 442 54 126
WYLY, CHIP USA 141

YOUNG, DAVID INDIANAPOLIS, IN 317 264 8000 91

ADWERBA AUSTRIA 140
AKIZUKI, SHIGERU TOKYO, JAPAN 03 3412 1371 203
AND (TRAFIC GRAFIC) BASEL, SWITZERLAND 061 271 2571 160
ANDERSON, CHARLES S., DESIGN CO. MINNEAPOLIS, MN 612 339 5181 72,
....79, 88, 109, 135, 183
AR&A ANTONIO ROMANO & ASSOCIATI ROME, ITALY 06 841 3001 ......108, 150
ART CENTER COLLEGE OF DESIGN OFFICE PASADENA, CA 818 584 5191 110
ASHBY DESIGN ANNAPOLIS, MD 410 263 4983 167

BAILEY LAUERMAN & ASSOCIATES LINCOLN, NE 402 475 2800 89
BATEY ADS SINGAPORE SINGAPORE 0322 0448 ....94, 133
BAUERS BÜRO GRÜNWALD, GERMANY 089 641 0091 ....58, 147, 162
BBV/MICHAEL BAVIERA ZURICH, SWITZERLAND 01 251 1755....120, 146, 147
BENES, PAVEL, GRAPHIC DESIGN PRAGUE, CZECH REPUBLIC 02 537 8083 .....
....116, 180
BITTER AGENTUR FÜR WERBUNG UND KOMMUNIKATION ....
HEIDELBERG, GERMANY 06221 484 456 31
BLECHMAN, R.O., INC. NEW YORK, NY 212 869 1630 55
BORGSTÄDT, BARBARA BENDESTORF, GERMANY 04183 6123 65
BROCK, MICHAEL, DESIGN LOS ANGELES, CA 213 932 0283 ....45, 48, 56
BROOKS CHAMPION INC. NEW YORK, NY 212 689 3620 30
BRUN UND BÜRGIN FOTOGRAFEN SWF ZURICH, SWITZERLAND 01 261 3538.....144
BUBBLAN, STUDIO BORAS, SWEDEN 033 114 441 51
BÜRO X HAMBURG, GERMANY 040 448 040-0 ....65, 144

CAMPBELL FISHER DITKO DESIGN PHOENIX, AZ 602 955 2707 30
CAPONE FRANCE 125
CARPENTER DESIGN NEW YORK, NY 212 431 6666 2
CARRUTHERS, ROY BROOKLYN, NY 718 965 1330 193
CARTER, DAVID, GRAPHIC DESIGN ASSOCIATES DALLAS, TX 214 826 4631 49
CENTO PER CENTO MILAN, ITALY 02 4801 2762 56
CHAN, ALAN, DESIGN COMPANY HONG KONG 0527 8228 ....135, 138, 139
CLARITY COVERDALE FURY ADVERTISING MINNEAPOLIS, MN 612 339 3902...140
CLARK, JOHN, STUDIO PROVIDENCE, RI 401 521 4678 25
CLEAVER ETAL LONDON, GREAT BRITAIN 081 566 2807 194
CLOCKWORK APPLE, INC. NEW YORK, NY 212 431 8996 ....93, 131
CN CORPORATION OSAKA, JAPAN 06 536 2371 ....102, 103
COOK AND SHANOSKY ASSOCIATES, INC. PRINCETON, NJ 609 452 1666 37
COREY MCPHERSON NASH WATERTOWN, MA 617 924 6050 112

CORNERSTONE DESIGN ASSOCIATES NEW YORK, NY 212 686 6046 156
CRESCENT LODGE DESIGN LONDON, GREAT BRITAIN 071 607 6733 49

DEMNER & MERLICEK VIENNA, AUSTRIA 01 588 46-0 ....42, 43
DENNARD CREATIVE, INC. DALLAS, TX 214 233 0430 36
DESIGN DEPT. PARIS, FRANCE 01 4285 2063 ....19, 108, 148, 174
DESIGN GUYS MINNEAPOLIS, MN 612 338 4462 100
DESIGNERELE KOMMUNIKATION GAUTING, GERMANY 089 850 8998 52
DESIGNWORKS WELLINGTON, NEW ZEALAND 04 384 6164 83
DOOKIM DESIGN SEOUL, KOREA 02 785 7599 ....151, 158, 159, 163
DUFFY, INC. MINNEAPOLIS, MN 612 339 3247 ....70, 75, 87
DYER, ROD, GROUP, INC. LOS ANGELES, CA 213 655 1800 175

ELEFANTEN & FARET AB, ATELJÉ STOCKHOLM, SWEDEN 08 301 502.....53, 151
EMERY VINCENT ASSOC. MELBOURNE, AUSTRALIA 03 699 3822...53, 71, 199

FALLON MCELLIGOTT MINNEAPOLIS, MN 612 332 2445 143
FELDER GRAFIK DESIGN RANKWEIL, AUSTRIA 05522 415 10-20 97
FFF, DIE WERBEAGENTUR HAMBURG, GERMANY 040 480 530 76
FOWLER, TOM, INC. STAMFORD, CT 203 329 1105 ....83, 96, 137, 154
FRANKFURT BALKIND PARTNERS NEW YORK, NY 212 421 5888 99

GGK WIEN WERBEAGENTUR VIENNA, AUSTRIA 01 940 505 136
GIBBS BARONET DALLAS, TX 214 954 0316 ....26, 185
GOOD, PETER, GRAPHIC DESIGN CHESTER, CT 203 526 9597 153
GORMAN, PAT, DESIGN NEW YORK, NY 212 620 0506 191
GRAFIKKEN HERNING, DENMARK 09721 4000 53
GROUP/CHICAGO, INC. CHICAGO, IL 312 787 4504 87

HAAG, BRUNO, KONZEPTION & ART DIRECTION ....
STUTTGART, GERMANY 0711 649 1215 41
HAMBLY & WOOLLEY INC. TORONTO, CANADA 416 504 2742.......57, 166, 172
HERNDON, KEN, GRAPHIC DESIGN LOUISVILLE, KY 502 451 6413 201
HETER-O-DOXY PROTPRAST OSAKA, JAPAN 06 535 1136 184
HIVELY AGENCY, THE, INC. HOUSTON, TX 713 961 2888 ....74, 128
HIXO, INC. AUSTIN, TX 512 477 0050 67
HOYNE, ANDREW, DESIGN MELBOURNE, AUSTRALIA 03 690 6458 170

IDENTICA LONDON, GREAT BRITAIN 071 221 9900 147
IMA-PRESS MOSCOW, RUSSIA 095 235 0949 155

INTÉGRAL RUEDI BAUR ET ASSOCIÉS MONTREUIL, FRANCE 01 4988 8050 . . . . 29, 152, 182

JORGENSEN, GRANT, DESIGN ADELAIDE, AUSTRALIA 08 271 7753 83

KENDALL-CHICAGO, DEWITT CHICAGO, IL 312 275 7884 44
KNOBEL, URS J., WERBUNG BAAR, SWITZERLAND 042 323 150 87
KUO DESIGN OFFICE NEW YORK, NY 212 343 9212 104
KYRAL, VERONIKA VIENNA, AUSTRIA 01 545 7174 . . . . 108, 110

LARSON DESIGN ASSOCIATES ROCKFORD, IL 815 229 0931 63
LEONHARDT GROUP, THE SEATTLE, WA 206 624 0551 123
LEUNG, JAMES, DESIGN BROOKLYN, NY 718 836 4695 107
LOOKING LOS ANGELES, CA 213 226 1086 77

M DESIGN LAUSANNE, SWITZERLAND 62
M PLUS M INCORPORATED NEW YORK, NY 212 807 0248 . . . . 92, 106, 117
MASTERS, ANNE, DESIGN, INC. WASHINGTON, DC 202 337 3748 27
MCCOOL & COMPANY MINNEAPOLIS, MN 612 332 3993 104
MCILHENNY COMPANY, DOMINO SUGAR USA 27
MENZE, LUTZ, DESIGN WUPPERTAL, GERMANY 0202 318 824 98
MERTEN DESIGN GROUP DENVER, CO 303 322 1451 79
MEYER & WALLIS MILWAUKEE, WI 414 224 0212 142
MILSTEIN, JEFF, STUDIO WOODSTOCK, NY 914 679 8403 . . . . 34, 35
MIRELEZ/ROSS INC. INDIANAPOLIS, IN 317 921 9753 118
MIRES DESIGN, INC. SAN DIEGO, CA 619 234 6631 . . . . 64, 79, 202
MODERN DOG SEATTLE, WA 206 282 8857 82
MORLA DESIGN SAN FRANCISCO, CA 415 543 6548 . . . . 54, 121
MULLER + COMPANY KANSAS CITY, MO 816 531 1992 101

NEWELL AND SORRELL LONDON, GREAT BRITAIN 071 722 1113 129

PARHAM SANTANA DESIGN NEW YORK, NY 212 645 7501 65
PENNEBAKER DESIGN HOUSTON, TX 713 963 8607 47
PENTAGRAM DESIGN SAN FRANCISCO, CA 415 981 6612 111
PERFACT WERBEAGENTUR DÜSSELDORF, GERMANY 0211 130 010 . . . . 38, 39
PETRICK DESIGN CHICAGO, IL 312 486 2880 105
PINKHAUS DESIGN CORP. MIAMI, FL 305 854 1000 . . . . 90, 91
PPA DESIGN LIMITED HONG KONG 0526 6991 . . . . 61, 157
PUSHPIN GROUP, THE NEW YORK, NY 212 674 8080 . . . . 40, 206

Q DESIGN GROUP, THE WILTON, CT 203 834 1885 4

RAIN MAKER ADVERTISING USA 165
RAPP COLLINS COMMUNICATIONS MINNEAPOLIS, MN 612 373 3000 . . . . . 78, 198
RICKABAUGH GRAPHICS GAHANNA, OH 614 337 2229 45

SABIN, TRACY, GRAPHIC DESIGN SAN DIEGO, CA 619 484 8712 135
SAMATA ASSOCIATES DUNDEE, IL 708 428 8600 24

SAYLES GRAPHIC DESIGN DES MOINES, IA 515 243 2922 23
SCHNEIDMAN, JARED, DESIGN NEW YORK, NY 212 475 2390 124
SHATZ, CAFÉ KONDITOREI SALZBURG, AUSTRIA 27
SIBLEY/PETEET DESIGN, INC. DALLAS, TX 214 761 9400 114
SIEGER DESIGN CONSULTING GMBH SASSENBERG, GERMANY 05426 9492-0 . 18
SILVER SMITH, JANE SYDNEY, AUSTRALIA 112
SIQUIS, LTD. BALTIMORE, MD 410 467 7300 130
601 DESIGN, INC. DENVER, CO 303 825 7913 186
SKETCH STUDIO PARIS, FRANCE 01 4321 8401 . . . . 46, 95, 115
SKJEI, M., (SHA) DESIGN CO. MINNEAPOLIS, MN 612 374 3528 32
SOMMESE DESIGN STATE COLLEGE, PA 814 238 7484 204
SPATCHURST DESIGN ASSOCIATES SYDNEY, AUSTRALIA 02 360 6755 . . . 22, 112
STIEHL/OTTE WERBEAGENTUR GMBH OSNABRÜCK, GERMANY 0541 258 859 . . 81
STUTZ, RALF OFFENBACH, GERMANY 069 816 161 86
SUN COMMUNICATIONS DESIGN MONTREAL, CANADA 514 521 5464 224
SWIETER DESIGN DALLAS, TX 214 720 6020 137

TAI-KEUNG, KAN, DESIGN & ASSOCIATES LTD. HONG KONG 0574 8399 21
TAM, JULIA, DESIGN PALOS VERDES, CA 310 378 7583 . . . . 60, 64
TAMMEN GMBH OSNABRÜCK, GERMANY 0541 940 0400 161
TARTAKOVER DESIGN TEL-AVIV, ISRAEL 03 517 3745 69
TESTA, ARMANDO, S.P.A. TORINO, ITALY 011 881 0111 146
TOLLESON DESIGN SAN FRANCISCO, CA 415 626 7796 127
TRADEMARK DESIGN (PTY) LTD. TRANSVAAL, SOUTH AFRICA 011 472 3642 . 73
TRIAD, INC. LARKSPUR, CA 415 925 3300 80
TRIBE! DESIGN HOUSTON, TX 713 523 5119 83
TRICKETT & WEBB LIMITED LONDON, GREAT BRITAIN 071 388 5832 . . . 20, 60
TUCKER DESIGN EASTWOOD, AUSTRALIA 08 373 0616 . . . . 73, 85, 87

ULMAJA, NINA, GRAFISK FORM STOCKHOLM, SWEDEN 08 612 7271 190
ULTIMO INC. NEW YORK, NY 212 645 7858 132
UNIVERS GMBH BERLIN, GERMANY 030 469 0090 177
UNOSAWA, KEISUKE, DESIGN TOKYO, JAPAN 03 5430 2154 . . . . 65, 68, 76, ... 122, 149, 188, 192, 200

VAUGHN WEDEEN CREATIVE ALBUQUERQUE, NM 505 243 4000 . . . . . 84, 87, 141
VISION & FACTORY GROOT-BIJGAARDEN, BELGIUM 02 466 5641 83

WIESE, BK, VISUAL DESIGN HAMBURG, GERMANY 040 603 8982 . . . . 33, 155
WIESMEIER, RG, WERBEAGENTUR GMBH MUNICH, GERMANY 089 290 089-0 . . . . 107, 108, 138
WONG & YEO, THE DESIGN OFFICE OF SAN FRANCISCO, CA 415 861 1128 . . 104
WURSTER, FRITZ W., INDUSTRIAL DESIGNERS . . . . WALDSTETTEN, GERMANY 07171 442 54 126

YOUNG & LARAMORE INDIANAPOLIS, IN 317 264 8000 91

(Z)OO PRODUKTIES, ERIC VAN CASTEREN, ROBERT VAN RIXTEL . . . . DEN HAAG, NETHERLANDS 070 364 2309 83

ADMINISTAFF USA..128
AGFA-COMPUGRAPHIC GERMANY......................177
AIGA LOS ANGELES LOS ANGELES, CA.................109
AIGA/LA LONG BEACH, CA..................................121
AMERICAN CENTER FOR DESIGN CHICAGO, IL.........109
AMERICAN MOVIE CLASSICS WOODBURY, NY..........99
AND (TRAFIC GRAFIC) BASEL, SWITZERLAND...........160
ANDERSON, CHARLES S., DESIGN CO. MINNEAPOLIS, MN.....72, 79
ANDRESEN TYPOGRAPHICS LOS ANGELES, CA.........175
ANGELI, PRIMO, INC. SAN FRANCISCO, CA.............66
AR&A ANTONIO ROMANO & ASSOCIATI ROME, ITALY..........150
ARCHITECTURAL RESOURCES CAMBRIDGE CAMBRIDGE, MA..........112
ART CENTER COLLEGE OF DESIGN PASADENA, CA......110
ART DIRECTORS ASSOCIATION OF IOWA DES MOINES, IA........109
ART GALLERY OF NEW SOUTH WALES SYDNEY, AUSTRALIA........112
AVON GRAPHICS DINGLEY, AUSTRALIA...................87

BATEY ADS SINGAPORE SINGAPORE...............94, 133
BAUERS BÜRO GRÜNWALD, GERMANY.................147
BEICH, KATHRYN (NESTLE-BEICH'S FUNDRAISING) BLOOMINGTON, IL.......78, 198
BIBERLE, REPROTECHNIK LEOBENSDORF, AUSTRIA......173
BMW AUSTRIA BANK AUSTRIA..........................140
BOISGIRARD, ETUDE PARIS, FRANCE..................125
BORDEAUX PRINTERS USA.............................79
BROCK, MICHAEL, DESIGN LOS ANGELES, CA.......48, 56
BRUN UND BÜRGIN FOTOGRAFEN SWF ZURICH, SWITZERLAND........144
BRUNO PHOTOGRAPHY INC. NEW YORK, NY.........165
BUBBLAN, STUDIO BORAS, SWEDEN....................51
BURKE & FOSTER PRINTING & COPYING DON MILLS, CANADA........172
BÜRO X HAMBURG, GERMANY......................65, 144
BUTLER ROGERS BASKETT NEW YORK, NY.............40
BZW-WERBEAGENTUR VIENNA, AUSTRIA.............107

CARMEN FURNITURE (SALES) PTY LIMITED MELBOURNE, AUSTRALIA.......71, 199
CARTER, DAVID, GRAPHIC DESIGN ASSOCIATES DALLAS, TX........49
CEHOVIN, EDUARD LJUBLJANA, SLOVENIA..............108
CONVATEC BRISTOL-MYERS GMBH MUNICH, GERMANY........138
COOK AND SHANOSKY ASSOCIATES, INC. PRINCETON, NJ........37
CORNERSTONE DESIGN ASSOCIATES NEW YORK, NY........156
COTTONG + TANIGUCHI USA..........................127
CRESCENT LODGE DESIGN LONDON, GREAT BRITAIN........49
CUTCARDS INC. STATE COLLEGE, PA...................204

DALLAS SOCIETY OF VISUAL COMMUNICATIONS DALLAS, TX........114
DEAN WITTER INTERNATIONAL NEW YORK, NY.............2
DEMNER & MERLICEK VIENNA, AUSTRIA............42, 43
DESIGNEREI F. KOMMUNIKATION GAUTING, GERMANY........52
DESIGNWORKS WELLINGTON, NEW ZEALAND............83
DEUTSCHE BANK BAUSPAR AG FRANKFURT/M., GERMANY........106

DIFFA (DESIGN INDUSTRY FOUNDATION FIGHTING AIDS) USA........105
DOMTAR SPECIALTY FINE PAPERS MONTREAL, CANADA........224
DOOKIM DESIGN SEOUL, KOREA............151, 158, 159, 163
DUFFY, INC. MINNEAPOLIS, MN......................70, 87

EBEL MONTRES SA LA CHAUX-DE-FONDS, SWITZERLAND........62
EDELMAN, TEDDY & ARTHUR, LTD. HAWLEYVILLE, CT........134
EISELEIN, MARTINA DÜSSELDORF, GERMANY.............68
ELEFANTEN & FARET AB, ATELJÉ STOCKHOLM, SWEDEN........53, 151
EMERY VINCENT ASSOCIATES MELBOURNE, AUSTRALIA........53

FACHHOCHSCHULE DÜSSELDORF DÜSSELDORF, GERMANY........93
FALLON MCELLIGOTT MINNEAPOLIS, MN 612 332 2445........143
FANCELLO, ANTONIO MILAN, ITALY...................186
FASHION STAGE GERMANY.............................58
FEILER, TOM, PHOTOGRAPHY TORONTO, CANADA........166
FINMECCANICA ROME, ITALY.........................108
FOLEY, KATE, COMPANY SAN FRANCISCO, CA.........104
FOWLER, TOM, INC. STAMFORD, CT...............96, 154
FOX RIVER PAPER COMPANY USA.......................75
FRENCH PAPER CO. MINNEAPOLIS, MN.................88
FRIEDMAN, ALAN/2424 BUILDING USA.............90, 91

GOLDEN HARVEST FILMS HONG KONG..................157
GOOD, JANET CHESTER, CT..........................153
GOOD, PETER CHESTER, CT..........................153
GRAFIKKEN HERNING, DENMARK........................53
GRAPHICS 3 JUPITER, FL.............................83
GRAY, COLIN GLASGOW, GREAT BRITAIN...............171
GRISS, MICHAEL RANKWEIL, AUSTRIA..................97
GRITZBACH, WERNER HAMBURG, GERMANY.............168
GROUP/CHICAGO, INC. CHICAGO, IL...................87
GUAREDISCH I. GERMANY.............................92

HAAG, BRUNO, KONZEPTION & ART DIRECTION STUTTGART, GERMANY........41
HACKETT, PAT, ARTIST REPRESENTATIVE SEATTLE, WA........123
HAMBLY & WOOLLEY INC. TORONTO, CANADA...........57
HARTZ, DANIEL KASTORF, GERMANY..................145
HEINE, DIRK GARBSEN, GERMANY....................164
HERRING MARATHON GROUP DALLAS, TX...............36
HERRON GALLERY USA...............................118
HIVELY AGENCY, THE, INC. HOUSTON, TX..............74
HIXO, INC. AUSTIN, TX..............................67
HORBER, J. ZURICH, SWITZERLAND...................146
HORTON PLAZA USA.................................135

IDENTICA LONDON, GREAT BRITAIN...................147
IMA-PRESS MOSCOW, RUSSIA.........................155
IMAGES HAIR SALON USA............................201

INDEPENDENT CURATORS INCORPORATED NEW YORK, NY 92, 106, 117
INK TANK, THE NEW YORK, NY 55
IRREGULAMADAIRE PARIS, FRANCE 148, 174

KANSAS CITY ART INSTITUTE KANSAS CITY, MO 101
KENDALL, DEWITT CHICAGO, IL 44
KOPPERL, HELGA USA 107
KOWLOON-CANTON RAILWAY CORPORATION HONG KONG 21
KUO DESIGN OFFICE NEW YORK, NY 104
KYRAL, LUDWIG, FA. VIENNA, AUSTRIA 108

LARSON DESIGN ASSOCIATES ROCKFORD, IL 63
LASALLE WHITAKER BROADVIEW, IL 109
LECOINTRE, DIDIER PARIS, FRANCE 46, 95, 115
LIMINTON CORCORAN DESIGN ADELAIDE, AUSTRALIA 83
LINIA GRAFIC MOSCOW, RUSSIA 176
LOOKING LOS ANGELES, CA 77
LOS ANGELES COUNTY MUSEUM OF ART LOS ANGELES, CA 119
LOVEN, PAUL, PHOTOGRAPHY, INC. PHOENIX, AZ 169

MANDARIN ORIENTAL HK, THE FLOWER SHOP HONG KONG 138, 139
MCCOOL, BARRY MINNEAPOLIS, MN 104
MERTEN DESIGN GROUP DENVER, CO 79
MEYER & WALLIS MILWAUKEE, WI 414 224 0212 142
MINISTRY OF THE ARTS AUSTRALIA 112
MINNESOTA PUBLIC RADIO ST. PAUL, MN 100
MIRES DESIGN, INC. SAN DIEGO, CA 64
MODERN DOG SEATTLE, WA 82
MORLA DESIGN SAN FRANCISCO, CA 54
MR. CHAN TEA ROOM LTD. HONG KONG 135
MTV USA 131
MUERMANN, HCH., GMBH & CO. KG INGOLSTADT, GERMANY 162
MUSEUM ARTS COUNCIL SAN FRANCISCO, CA 111
MUSEUM OF MODERN ART NEW YORK, NY 34, 35
MYERS, BARRY SILVER SPRING, MD 167

NEW CANAAN SOCIETY FOR THE ARTS USA 4
NORTHWESTERN NATIONAL LIFE USA 140

OP COUTURE BRILLEN GMBH MUNICH, GERMANY 107
ORDER OF THE GLOBE USA 23
OSAKA GAS RESEARCH INSTITUTE FOR CULTURE, ENERGY AND LIFE (CEL) ....
OSAKA, JAPAN 102, 103
OZANNE, DENIS PARIS, FRANCE 46, 95, 115

PANAMA JACK BARCELONA, SPAIN 108
PAPER HOUSE PRODUCTIONS USA 196, 197
PARHAM SANTANA DESIGN NEW YORK, NY 65
PENNEBAKER DESIGN HOUSTON, TX 47
PERFACT WERBEAGENTUR DÜSSELDORF, GERMANY 38, 39
PORSCHE AUSTRIA GESMBH & CO. SALZBURG, AUSTRIA 136
PPA DESIGN LIMITED HONG KONG 61
PRINT CRAFT, INC. NEW BRIGHTON, MN 88
PUSHPIN ASSOCIATES, THE NEW YORK, NY 212 674 8080 206

RICKABAUGH GRAPHICS GAHANNA, OH 45
ROMAGNOLI, MARIA CRISTINA ROME, ITALY 59

SAN FRANCISCO ARCHITECTURAL FOUNDATION SAN FRANCISCO, CA ...111
SAN FRANCISCO MOMA SAN FRANCISCO, CA 111

SCHIRMER, HEIKE DÜSSELDORF, GERMANY 68
SCHWAB COMPANY, THE NEW YORK, NY 130
SEKRETARIAT FÜR GEMEINSAME KULTURARBEIT IN NRW WUPPERTAL, GERMANY 98
SIEGER DESIGN SASSENBERG, GERMANY 18
SINGAPORE AIRLINES SINGAPORE 133
SKJEI, M., (SHA) DESIGN CO. MINNEAPOLIS, MN 32
SOLID AUDIO PURKERSDORF, AUSTRIA 62
SONY MUSIC ENTERTAINMENT INC. NEW YORK, NY 99
STAFF P.E.L. ET CALYPSO PARIS, FRANCE 108
STANDARD ARCHITECTUR PARIS, FRANCE 19
STIEHL/OTTE WERBEAGENTUR GMBH OSNABRÜCK, GERMANY 81
STUTZ, RALF OFFENBACH, GERMANY 86
SUN STUDIO MELBOURNE, AUSTRALIA 170
SYDNEY ELECTRICITY SYDNEY, AUSTRALIA 22

T & O TREUHAND REGENSDORF, SWITZERLAND 147
TAM, JULIA, DESIGN PALOS VERDES, CA 60, 64
TAMMEN GMBH OSNABRÜCK, GERMANY 161
TARTAKOVER, DAVID TEL-AVIV, ISRAEL 69
TERRANO SCHUH GMBH ROSSWEIN, GERMANY 76
TESTA, ARMANDO, S.P.A. TORINO, ITALY 146
THOMSON C.E. INDIANAPOLIS, IN 135
TRADEMARK DESIGN (PTY) LTD. TRANSVAAL, SOUTH AFRICA 73
TRIAD, INC. LARKSPUR, CA 80
TRIBE! DESIGN HOUSTON, TX 83
TRICKETT & WEBB LIMITED LONDON, GREAT BRITAIN 20, 60
TUCKER DESIGN EASTWOOD, AUSTRALIA 73
TURNER CLASSIC MOVIES ATLANTA, GA 135
TÜV RHEINLAND IBÉRICA S.A. SPAIN 151

UHLMANN GRAPHICDESIGNERS WARTHAUSEN, GERMANY 74
ULTIMO INC. NEW YORK, NY 132
UNION RAILWAYS LIMITED CROYDON, GREAT BRITAIN 129
UNOSAWA, KEISUKE, DESIGN TOKYO, JAPAN 65, 68, 76, 122, 149, 200
US WEST COMMUNICATIONS PHOENIX, AZ 141

VAUGHN WEDEEN CREATIVE ALBUQUERQUE, NM 505 243 4000 ....84, 87
VICTORIA WERKE AG, MÖBELFABRIK SWITZERLAND 87
VISION & FACTORY GROOT-BIJGAARDEN, BELGIUM 83

WACHSMANN VIENNA, AUSTRIA 110
WAGNEROVA, IRENA CZECH REPUBLIC 116
WARNER HOME VIDEO USA 45
WEIHS, SASCHA BIBERACH, GERMANY 149
WEST THAMES COLLEGE LONDON, GREAT BRITAIN 113
WESTERN PAPER COMPANY LINCOLN, NE 89
WIESE, BRUNO HAMBURG, GERMANY 33, 155
WIESE, RUTH HAMBURG, GERMANY 33, 155
WILHELM CONSTRUCTION INDIANAPOLIS, IN 91
WOHNFLEX ZÜRICH ZURICH, SWITZERLAND 120
WOODS BAGOT ADELAIDE, AUSTRALIA 85
WOODS, H.T. CRANSTON, RI 137
WURSTER, FRITZ W., INDUSTRIAL DESIGNERS WALDSTETTEN, GERMANY 126

YÉ DESIGN JINAN, CHINA 205
YOUNG PRESIDENTS' ORGANIZATION USA 137

(Z)OO PRODUKTIES, ERIC VAN CASTEREN, ROBERT VAN RIXTEL ....
DEN HAAG, NETHERLANDS 83

CALL FOR ENTRIES

EINLADUNG

APPEL D'ENVOIS

CALL FOR ENTRIES

E N T R Y   F O R M

I wish to enter the attached in the following Graphis competition:

□ **GRAPHIS POSTER 96** (DEADLINE APRIL 30, 1995)
CATEGORY CODES/KATEGORIEN/CATÉGORIES
□ **PO1**   ADVERTISING/WERBUNG/PUBLICITÉ
□ **PO2**   PROMOTION
□ **PO3**   CULTURE/KULTUR
□ **PO4**   SOCIAL/GESELLSCHAFT/SOCIÉTÉ

□ **GRAPHIS PHOTO 96** (DEADLINE AUGUST 31, 1995)
CATEGORY CODES/KATEGORIEN/CATÉGORIES
□ **PH1**   FASHION/MODE
□ **PH2**   JOURNALISM/JOURNALISMUS
□ **PH3**   STILL LIFE/STILLEBEN/NATURE MORTE
□ **PH4**   FOOD/LEBENSMITTEL/CUISINE
□ **PH5**   PEOPLE/MENSCHEN/PERSONNES
□ **PH6**   PRODUCTS/PRODUKTE/PRODUITS
□ **PH7**   LANDSCAPES/LANDSCHAFTEN/EXTÉRIEURS
□ **PH8**   ARCHITECTURE/ARCHITEKTUR
□ **PH9**   WILD LIFE/TIERE/ANIMAUX
□ **PH10** SPORTS/SPORT
□ **PH11** FINE ART/KUNST/ART

□ **GRAPHIS DESIGN 97** (DEADLINE NOVEMBER 30, 1995)
CATEGORY CODES/KATEGORIEN/CATÉGORIES
□ **DE1**   ADVERTISING/WERBUNG/ PUBLICITÉ
□ **DE2**   BOOKS/BÜCHER/LIVRES
□ **DE3**   BROCHURES/BROSCHÜREN
□ **DE4**   CALENDARS/KALENDER/CALENDRIERS
□ **DE5**   CORPORATE IDENTITY
□ **DE6**   EDITORIAL/REDAKTIONELL/RÉDACTIONNEL
□ **DE7**   ILLUSTRATION
□ **DE8**   PACKAGING/VERPACKUNG
□ **DE9**   MISCELLANEOUS/ANDERE/DIVERS

SIGNATURE:

SENDER:

COMPANY, ADDRESS

TELEPHONE   FAX

ART DIRECTOR:

ADDRESS

TELEPHONE   FAX

DESIGNER:

ADDRESS

TELEPHONE   FAX

PHOTOGRAPHER:

ADDRESS

TELEPHONE   FAX

ILLUSTRATOR:

ADDRESS

TELEPHONE   FAX

AGENCY, STUDIO:

ADDRESS

TELEPHONE   FAX

CLIENT:

ADDRESS

G R A P H I S   B O O K S

BOOK ORDER FORM: USA, CANADA, SOUTH AMERICA, ASIA, PACIFIC

BOOKS	ALL REGIONS
☐ GRAPHIS ALTERNATIVE PHOTOGRAPHY 95	US$ 69.00
☐ GRAPHIS PACKAGING 6	US$ 75.00
☐ GRAPHIS DESIGN 95	US$ 69.00
☐ GRAPHIS ADVERTISING 95	US$ 69.00
☐ GRAPHIS BROCHURES 1	US$ 75.00
☐ GRAPHIS PAPER PROMOTIONS	US$ 69.00
☐ GRAPHIS PRODUCTS BY DESIGN	US$ 69.00
☐ GRAPHIS TYPOGRAPHY 1	US$ 75.00
☐ GRAPHIS PHOTO 94	US$ 69.00
☐ GRAPHIS NUDES	US$ 85.00
☐ GRAPHIS POSTER 95	US$ 69.00
☐ GRAPHIS T-SHIRT 1	US$ 75.00
☐ GRAPHIS CORPORATE IDENTITY 2	US$ 75.00
☐ GRAPHIS LETTERHEAD 2	US$ 69.00
☐ GRAPHIS LOGO 2	US$ 60.00
☐ GRAPHIS ANNUAL REPORTS 4	US$ 75.00
☐ GRAPHIS PUBLICATION 1 (ENGLISH)	US$ 75.00
☐ ART FOR SURVIVAL: THE ILLUSTRATOR AND THE ENVIRONMENT	US$ 45.00

NOTE! NY RESIDENTS ADD 8.25% SALES TAX

☐ CHECK ENCLOSED (PAYABLE TO GRAPHIS)
(US$ ONLY, DRAWN ON A BANK IN THE USA)

USE CREDIT CARDS (DEBITED IN US DOLLARS)

☐ AMERICAN EXPRESS   ☐ MASTERCARD   ☐ VISA

CARD NO. _____ EXP. DATE _____

CARDHOLDER NAME _____

SIGNATURE _____

☐ PLEASE BILL ME (BOOK(S) WILL BE SENT WHEN PAYMENT IS RECEIVED)

(PLEASE PRINT)

NAME _____

TITLE _____

COMPANY _____

ADDRESS _____

CITY _____

STATE/PROVINCE _____ ZIP CODE _____

COUNTRY _____

SEND ORDER FORM AND MAKE CHECK PAYABLE TO:
GRAPHIS US, INC.,
141 LEXINGTON AVENUE, NEW YORK, NY 10016-8193, USA

BOOK ORDER FORM: EUROPE, AFRICA, MIDDLE EAST

BOOKS	EUROPE/AFRICA MIDDLE EAST	GERMANY	U.K.
☐ ALTERNATIVE PHOTO 95	SFR.123.–	DM 149,–	£ 52.00
☐ GRAPHIS PACKAGING 6	SFR.137.–	DM 162,–	£ 55.00
☐ GRAPHIS DESIGN 95	SFR.123.–	DM 149,–	£ 52.00
☐ GRAPHIS ADVERTISING 95	SFR.123.–	DM 149,–	£ 52.00
☐ GRAPHIS BROCHURES 1	SFR.137.–	DM 162,–	£ 55.00
☐ PAPER PROMOTIONS	SFR.123.–	DM 149,–	£ 52.00
☐ PRODUCTS BY DESIGN	SFR.123.–	DM 149,–	£ 52.00
☐ GRAPHIS TYPOGRAPHY 1	SFR.137.–	DM 162,–	£ 55.00
☐ GRAPHIS PHOTO 94	SFR.123.–	DM 149,–	£ 52.00
☐ GRAPHIS NUDES	SFR.168.–	DM 168,–	£ 62.00
☐ GRAPHIS POSTER 95	SFR.123.–	DM 149,–	£ 52.00
☐ GRAPHIS T-SHIRT 1	SFR.137.–	DM 162,–	£ 55.00
☐ CORPORATE IDENTITY 2	SFR.137.–	DM 162,–	£ 55.00
☐ GRAPHIS LETTERHEAD 2	SFR.123.–	DM 149,–	£ 52.00
☐ GRAPHIS LOGO 2	SFR. 92.–	DM 108,–	£ 38.00
☐ ANNUAL REPORTS 4	SFR.137.–	DM 162,–	£ 55.00
☐ GRAPHIS PUBLICATION 1 ☐ ENGLISH ☐ GERMAN	SFR.137.–	DM 162,–	£ 55.00
☐ ART FOR SURVIVAL: THE ILLUSTRATOR AND THE ENVIRONMENT	SFR. 79.–	DM 89,–	£ 35.00

(FOR ORDERS FROM EC COUNTRIES V.A.T. WILL BE CHARGED IN ADDITION TO ABOVE BOOK PRICES)

FOR CREDIT CARD PAYMENT (DEBITED IN SWISS FRANCS):

☐ AMERICAN EXPRESS   ☐ DINER'S CLUB
☐ VISA/BARCLAYCARD/CARTE BLEUE

CARD NO. _____ EXP. DATE _____

CARDHOLDER NAME _____

SIGNATURE _____

☐ PLEASE BILL ME (ADDITIONAL MAILING COSTS WILL BE CHARGED)

(PLEASE PRINT)

LAST NAME _____ FIRST NAME _____

TITLE _____

COMPANY _____

ADDRESS _____

CITY _____ POSTAL CODE _____

COUNTRY _____

PLEASE SEND ORDER FORM TO:
GRAPHIS PRESS CORP.
DUFOURSTRASSE 107
CH–8008 ZÜRICH, SWITZERLAND

G R A P H I S   M A G A Z I N E